THE MERCHANT
OF VENICE

SHAKESPEARE AT STRATFORD

Published by The Arden Shakespeare in association with
The Shakespeare Birthplace Trust

General Editor: Robert Smallwood, The Shakespeare Centre

Associate Editors: Susan Brock, The Shakespeare Centre Library
Russell Jackson, The Shakespeare Institute

KING RICHARD III   *Gillian Day*
THE MERCHANT OF VENICE   *Miriam Gilbert*
THE WINTER'S TALE   *Patricia E. Tatspaugh*

Forthcoming titles:
ROMEO AND JULIET   *Russell Jackson*
THE TEMPEST   *David Lindley*
AS YOU LIKE IT   *Robert Smallwood*

SHAKESPEARE AT STRATFORD

THE MERCHANT OF VENICE

MIRIAM GILBERT

The Arden website is at
http://www.ardenshakespeare.com

Shakespeare at Stratford: *The Merchant of Venice*
first published 2002 by The Arden Shakespeare
in association with the Shakespeare Birthplace Trust

© 2002 Miriam Gilbert

Arden Shakespeare is an imprint of Thomson Learning

Thomson Learning
Berkshire House
168-173 High Holborn
London WC1V 7AA

Typeset by LaserScript, Mitcham, Surrey

Printed by Zrinski in Croatia

British Library Cataloguing in Publication Data
A catalogue record for this book is available from the British Library

Library of Congress Cataloguing in Publication Data
A catalogue record has been applied for

ISBN 1-903436-13-3 (pbk)
NPN 9 8 7 6 5 4 3 2 1

THE AUTHOR

Miriam Gilbert is a Professor of English at the University of Iowa, where she has taught since 1969. Her publications include *Shakespeare in Performance: Love's Labour's Lost* (1993), *Stages of Drama* (drama anthology, now in its fourth edition), and a series of essays on performance and teaching. She has directed eight seminars for teachers, both secondary and college, on 'Shakespeare: Text and Theatre' under the auspices of the National Endowment for the Humanities; she also serves as a visiting lecturer at the Shakespeare Centre in Stratford-upon-Avon.

THE AUTHOR

CONTENTS

List of illustrations **viii**
General editor's preface **xii**
Acknowledgements **xiv**

Introduction 1

1 SHYLOCK 25

2 THE VENETIANS 44

3 THE PROBLEM OF LAUNCELOT GOBBO 67

4 BELMONT 80

5 SHYLOCK THE JEW 106

6 THE TRIAL 117

7 BELMONT REVISITED 145

APPENDICES
1 Production credits and cast lists 158
2 Reviews cited 172
3 Abbreviations 175

Bibliography **177**
Index **179**

LIST OF ILLUSTRATIONS

1 **1.3:** Antonio, Shylock and Bassanio, 1956
   Photograph: Angus McBean **5**

2 **1.3:** Tubal, Shylock, Antonio and Bassanio, 1993
   Photograph: Malcolm Davies **7**

3 **1.3:** Shylock, Antonio and Bassanio, 1987
   Photograph: Joe Cocks Studio **29**

4 **1.3:** Bassanio, Antonio and Shylock, 1978
   Photograph: Joe Cocks Studio **32**

5 **2.5:** Jessica, Shylock and Launcelot Gobbo, 1981
   Photograph: Joe Cocks Studio **37**

6 **2.5:** Shylock and Jessica, 1993
   Photograph: Alistair Muir **41**

7 **First Venice setting**, 1956
   Photograph: Peter Streuli **45**

8 **Set, 1.1:** with table forestage, 1993
   Photograph: Malcolm Davies **46**

9 **1.1:** Antonio, Gratiano, Lorenzo and Bassanio, 1993
   Photograph: Malcolm Davies **48**

10 **1.1:** Antonio and Bassanio, 1971
    Photograph: Joe Cocks Studio **49**

11 **1.1:** Bassanio and Antonio, 1997
    Photograph: Malcolm Davies **52**

12 **2.6:** Lorenzo, Gratiano, Jessica, Salarino and masquers 1947
    Photograph: Angus McBean **60**

13 **3.1:** Salerio, Shylock and Solanio, 1987
    Photograph: Joe Cocks Studio **65**

14 **2.2:** Launcelot Gobbo, 1978
    Photograph: Joe Cocks Studio **70**

15 **2.2:** Launcelot Gobbo, 1993
    Photograph: Alistair Muir **73**

16   2.2: Launcelot Gobbo, 1987
     Photograph: Joe Cocks Studio   **74**

17   3.5: Jessica and Launcelot Gobbo, 1971
     Photograph: Donald Cooper   **77**

18   1.2: Portia and Nerissa, 1997
     Photograph: Malcolm Davies   **87**

19   2.7: Portia and Morocco, 1981
     Photograph: Joe Cocks Studio   **88**

20   **2.7 or 2.9:** Nerissa, Arragon, Portia and caskets, 1971
     Photograph: Thomas Holte   **89**

21   **Set**, with caskets in raised position, 1984
     Photograph: Joe Cocks Studio   **90**

22   2.7: Morocco and Portia, 1960
     Photograph, Thomas Holte   **94**

23   2.9: Tutor, attendants, Mother to Arragon, Arragon, Servant,
     Stephano, Portia, Nerissa and attendants above, 1960
     Photograph: Angus McBean   **97**

24   3.2: Bassanio, Balthazar, Gratiano, Portia and Nerissa, 1987
     Photograph: Joe Cocks Studio   **102**

25   3.1: Solanio, Salerio and Shylock, 1997
     Photograph: Malcolm Davies   **109**

26   3.1: Tubal and Shylock, 1978
     Photograph: Joe Cocks Studio   **112**

27   3.1: Tubal and Shylock, 1960
     Photograph: Angus McBean   **113**

28   4.1: Salerio, Solanio, Gratiano, Portia, Antonio, Bassanio,
     Nerissa, Shylock and Duke, 1960
     Photograph: Angus McBean   **119**

29   4.1: Officer, Antonio, Portia and Shylock, 1965
     Photograph: Thomas Holte   **123**

30   4.1: Salerio, Shylock, Gaoler and Portia, 1986
     Photograph: Michael Le Poer Trench   **124**

31   4.1: Clerk, Shylock, Duke, Nerissa and Portia, 1953
     Photograph: Angus McBean   **128**

32 **4.1:** Gratiano, Shylock, Duke, Portia, Nerissa, Solanio,
    Antonio, Gaoler, Bassanio and Salerio, 1953
    Photograph: Angus McBean **131**

33 **4.1:** Bassanio, Antonio, Clerk of the Court, Priest, Duke,
    Nerissa, Portia, Shylock, Solanio and Gratiano, 1956
    Photograph: Angus McBean **132**

34 **4.1:** Antonio and Solanio, 1978
    Photograph: Joe Cocks Studio **133**

35 **4.1:** Shylock and Antonio, 1971
    Photograph: Reg Wilson **134**

36 **4.1:** Bassanio, Gratiano, Salerio, Solanio, Shylock, Antonio
    and Officer, 1993
    Photograph: Malcolm Davies **136**

37 **4.1:** Shylock, 1997
    Photograph: Malcolm Davies **141**

38 **5.1:** Lorenzo and Jessica, 1953
    Photograph: Angus McBean **147**

39 **5.1:** Bassanio, Portia, Launcelot Gobbo, Servant, Lorenzo,
    Antonio, Jessica, Nerissa and Gratiano, 1981
    Photograph: Joe Cocks Studio. **155**

40 **5.1:** Antonio, Jessica, Lorenzo, Bassanio, Portia, Nerissa and
    Gratiano, 1956
    Photograph: Angus McBean **156**

Cover photographs
Shylock, played by Antony Sher, 1987, and David Suchet,
1981
Photographs: Ivan Kyncl (Sher), Donald Cooper (Suchet)

SOURCES
Joe Cocks Studio: The Joe Cocks Studio Collection, The Shakespeare Centre
Library, Stratford-upon-Avon
Malcolm Davies: The Shakespeare Centre Library, Stratford-upon-Avon
Thomas Holte: The Tom Holte Theatre Photographic Collection, The
Shakespeare Centre Library, Stratford-upon-Avon

Angus McBean and Reg Wilson: The Royal Shakespeare Company Collection, The Shakespeare Centre Library, Stratford-upon-Avon
Donald Cooper
Ivan Kyncl
Michael Le Poer Trench
Alistair Muir
Peter Streuli

Every effort has been made to contact copyright holders and the publishers will be happy to include further acknowledgements.

GENERAL EDITOR'S PREFACE

The theatre archive housed in the Shakespeare Centre Library here in Stratford-upon-Avon is among the most important in the world; for the study of the performance history of Shakespeare's plays in the twentieth century it is unsurpassed. It covers the entire period from the opening of Stratford's first Shakespeare Memorial Theatre in 1879, through its replacement, following the fire of 1926, by the present 1932 building (renamed the Royal Shakespeare Theatre in 1961) and the addition of the studio theatre (The Other Place) in 1974 and of the Swan Theatre in 1986, and it becomes fuller as the years go by. The archive's collection of promptbooks, press reviews, photographs in their hundreds of thousands, and, over the last couple of decades, archival video recordings, as well as theatre programmes, costume designs, stage managers' performance reports, and a whole range of related material, provides the Shakespeare theatre historian with a remarkably rich and concentrated body of material. The wealth and accessibility of this collection have sometimes tended to give general performance histories of Shakespeare's plays an unintentional Stratford bias; the aim of the Shakespeare at Stratford series is to exploit, and indeed revel in, the archive's riches.

Each volume in the series covers the Stratford performance history of a Shakespeare play since World War II. The record of performances at Stratford's various theatres through this period unquestionably offers a wider, fuller and more various range of productions than is provided by any other single theatre company. It may fairly be said, therefore, that a study of the Stratford productions since 1945 of any Shakespeare play provides a representative cross-section of the main trends in its theatrical interpretation in the second half of the twentieth century. Each volume in the Shakespeare at Stratford series will, however, begin with an introduction that sets this Stratford half-century in the wider context of the main trends of its play's performance history before this period and of significant productions elsewhere during it.

The organization of individual volumes is, of course, the responsibility of their authors, though within the general aim of the series to avoid mere chronicling. No volume in the series will therefore offer a chronological account of the Stratford productions of its play: some will group together for consideration and analysis productions of similar or comparable style or approach; others will examine individual aspects or sections of their plays across the whole range of the half-century of Stratford productions' treatment of them. Illustrations are chosen for what they demonstrate about a particular production choice, a decision that, on some occasions, may be more important than photographic quality. Given the frequency with which individual plays return, in entirely new productions, to the Stratford repertoire, most volumes in the series will have some ten or even a dozen productions' approaches and choices to consider and contrast, a range that will provide a vivid sense of the extraordinary theatrical diversity and adaptability of Shakespeare's plays.

The conception and planning of this series would not have been possible without the support and enthusiasm of Sylvia Morris and Marian Pringle of the Shakespeare Centre Library, Kathy Elgin, Head of Publications at the Royal Shakespeare Company, Jessica Hodge and her colleagues at the Arden Shakespeare, and above all, my two Associate Editors, Susan Brock of the Shakespeare Centre Library and Russell Jackson of the Shakespeare Institute. To all of them I am deeply grateful.

ROBERT SMALLWOOD
The Shakespeare Centre, Stratford-upon-Avon

ACKNOWLEDGEMENTS

The theatre is essentially a collaborative enterprise, and, not surprisingly, this book owes its existence to the support of many individuals. I am particularly grateful for financial support from the Jubilee Education Fund of the Shakespeare Birthplace Trust and a Faculty Developmental Leave from the University of Iowa. The time for research created through these grants was spent most happily at the Shakespeare Centre Library where the expertise of librarians Marian Pringle, Susan Brock and Karin Brown, and the detailed knowledge of RSC Production Manager (now retired) Roger Howells helped me with issues both large and small; RSC Librarian Sylvia Morris has been a long-time adviser, consultant and finder of pertinent materials. My friend and colleague Patricia Tatspaugh has encouraged me generously over the past years, and has shared her own writing with me. Conversations, either in writing or in person, with actors lie behind some of the details recorded here, and I wish to thank Judy Buxton, David Calder, Avril Carson, Tony Church, Alison Fiske, Rachel Joyce, David Suchet and Philip Voss for their insights. Many of my ideas about the play come from the performances I've seen, but also from the scholarly articles and editions I've consulted, particularly the critical editions of J.R. Brown, Jay C. Halio and M.M. Mahood, and the superb study of the play in performance by James C. Bulman. The support of those connected with the publication process – Jessica Hodge, Hannah Hyam, Judith Ravenscroft and Andrew McAleer – has been full, patient and extremely helpful. My greatest thanks go to Robert Smallwood, whose generosity, humour and intelligence have guided me, and my students, through hours of delightful conversation. This book grows out of my own theatre-going, reading and research, but it is shaped by Robert Smallwood's questions and his elegantly detailed writing about a subject we both love, Shakespeare in performance.

MIRIAM GILBERT

Iowa City, August 2001

INTRODUCTION

The Merchant of Venice shares with *Hamlet* the distinction of having
been more often performed than any other of Shakespeare's plays.
M.M. Mahood, Introduction to the New Cambridge
Shakespeare edition (1987) of the play

It is often suggested that a closed season should be declared on some
of Shakespeare's plays, and *The Merchant of Venice* would probably
qualify for early inclusion.
Clifford Williams, director of the 1965 Royal Shakespeare
Company production of the play, programme note

These contrasting statements about the 'playability' of
The Merchant of Venice point directly to the questions
which both enliven this play and make it the subject
of frequent attacks. Is Shylock a nasty villain or the victim of
religious prejudice – or both? Is Portia a rich, condescending
heiress or a young woman trapped by her dead father's orders –
or both? Is Bassanio a scheming fortune-hunter or an ardent if
thoughtless lover or a careless exploiter of his friend's fortune?
Is Antonio a generous, self-sacrificing gentleman or a deliberately guilt-inducing martyr? Does Jessica run away from her
father because she hates him, or because she hates being a Jew?
Does she exchange the ring her mother gave her father as a
conscious rejection (she is buying a monkey) or is it simply
thoughtlessness?

The Merchant of Venice is therefore a play of questions, both those asked within the play and those it insistently raises for actors, directors, designers and audiences. The opening line, 'In sooth I know not why I am so sad', is an indirect and perhaps never answered question. Antonio interrogates Bassanio: 'tell me now what lady is the same / To whom you swore a secret pilgrimage' (1.1.119–20). The riddles posed by the three caskets and their inscriptions are questions. Scene after scene develops through questions. Bassanio, desperate for money so that he may go and woo Portia, asks Shylock, 'May you stead me? Will you pleasure me? Shall I know your answer?' (1.3.6–7). And when Antonio asks again, somewhat later in the same scene, 'Well Shylock, shall we be beholding to you?' (100) he receives not an answer but a powerful series of ironic and ever longer questions:

> What should I say to you? Should I not say
> 'Hath a dog money? is it possible
> A cur can lend three thousand ducats?' or
> Shall I bend low and in a bondman's key,
> With bated breath and whisp'ring humbleness,
> Say this:
> 'Fair sir, you spat on me on Wednesday last,
> You spurn'd me such a day, another time
> You call'd me dog; and for these courtesies
> I'll lend you thus much moneys'?
>
> (1.3.115–24)

Even Launcelot Gobbo's stand-up comedy routine about his conscience and the fiend is a debate between conflicting voices – which one will he listen to? And the following sequence, with his old blind father repeatedly asking 'which is the way to Master Jew's?' and then 'Talk you of young Master Launcelot?', is built on questions, with the last and most important being 'Do you not know me father?' (2.2.31–2, 46–7, 70).

Indeed, questions about identity are everywhere in the play, even when they seem merely cues to get an actor on stage. '[W]ho is he comes here?' (1.3.34) asks Shylock as Antonio approaches.

'Who are you? – tell me for more certainty, / Albeit I'll swear that I do know your tongue' (2.6.26–7), asks Jessica, as she looks out from the 'above' area, waiting for Lorenzo to help her escape from her father's house. 'Did I deserve no more than a fool's head? / Is that my prize? are my deserts no better?' asks the disappointed Prince of Arragon after opening the silver casket and finding not Portia's picture but 'the portrait of a blinking idiot' (2.9.59–60, 54). And when Shylock launches into his passionate explanation of his decision to follow through with his revenge on Antonio, he does so in a magnificently structured series of questions:

> Hath not a Jew eyes? hath not a Jew hands, organs, dimensions, senses, affections, passions? fed with the same food, hurt with the same weapons, subject to the same diseases, healed by the same means, warmed and cooled by the same winter and summer as a Christian is? – if you prick us do we not bleed? if you tickle us do we not laugh? if you poison us do we not die? and if you wrong us shall we not revenge? – if we are like you in the rest, we will resemble you in that. If a Jew wrong a Christian, what is his humility? Revenge! If a Christian wrong a Jew, what should his sufferance be by Christian example? – why revenge! The villainy you teach me I will execute, and it shall go hard but I will better the instruction. (3.1.52–66)

One of the many factors which makes this an effective speech is its ability to trap the listener into responding 'yes' – yes, a Jew has eyes, hands, organs; yes, a Jew shares physical commonality with Christians, bleeding, laughing, dying. And thus, the listener feels forced to continue agreeing that a Jew's 'sufferance' – his patience or forbearance – will, necessarily because of the rhetorical sequence so thoroughly prepared, become 'revenge'. There's no way out.

Yet of all these questions, the one which has always intrigued me most is Portia's question when she enters the court, disguised as a lawyer. First she too is questioned: 'come you from old Bellario?' and 'Are you acquainted with the difference / That holds this present question in the court?' (4.1.165, 167–8). She claims, 'I am informed throughly of the cause' – she's totally briefed – and then she says, 'Which is the merchant here? and which the Jew?' (169–70). It's another one of those identity questions and yet it's much more wide-reaching in its implications. On the page, the question is simple. But as soon as we think in stage terms, we immediately see the problem. How can Portia *not* know which is which? Isn't Shylock immediately recognizable by his 'Jewish gaberdine' (1.3.107)? Isn't his difference always apparent, under-lined by the constant reference to him or addressing of him as Jew (the words 'Jew' and 'Jewish' appear sixty-nine times in the text, while Shylock's name appears seventeen times)?

To ask this question in relation to the staging opens up a variety of possible answers. If Shylock looks clearly alien (Figure 1), differentiated by style of clothing, or a beard of biblical proportions, or long hair perhaps with the traditional side-curls, or a particular distinguishing badge, a Portia will have to decide how to make sense of the line. Is she, perhaps, not looking at the two men at all, busying herself with getting papers out or stacking up lawbooks? Are there lots of people on stage, perhaps a group of Venetians and a group of Jews, so that it's not clear who is Antonio and who is Shylock? That's one possible implication of the Duke's follow-up to her question, 'Antonio and old Shylock, both stand forth' (4.1.171). Or is she putting on a mask of scrupulous impartiality?

Or, and here the question implies a very different staging choice, is it possible that she really *can't* tell the difference at all? Are Shylock and Antonio visually very similar – and we must remember that while we, as audience, have been watching these two men for some time, Portia has never seen them before. Are they roughly the same age? Are they wearing similar clothes? In 1970, when Jonathan Miller directed *The Merchant of Venice* at London's National Theatre, with Laurence Olivier as Shylock, the set evoked late nineteenth-century Venice, and both Antonio and Shylock were white-haired, clean-shaven, elegant gentlemen; they wore top hats, which they courteously tipped to each other, as well as long frock coats and striped trousers. Only the yarmulke visible under the top hat showed, outwardly, Shylock's 'difference'. And

FIGURE 1 Against a background suggesting Renaissance Venice, Antonio (Anthony Nicholls) agrees to Shylock's (Emlyn Williams) conditions while Bassanio (Basil Hoskins) watches. Shylock's Mogen David is just visible on his chest. (1.3, 1956)

the Royal Shakespeare Company has offered similar approaches, most notably in 1981, when John Barton's production on the main stage at Stratford with David Suchet as Shylock gave us a well-dressed, cigar-smoking, jovial Shylock (see cover). The fur collar on his coat marked his wealth, as did Antonio's, and here the difference was visible primarily because Shylock was bearded and Antonio wasn't. Later, in the touring version of 1986, Nigel Terry's Shylock was surprisingly young, perhaps even younger than Paul Webster's Antonio, but both wore similar Victorian coats and trousers. In 1993, David Thacker's production set in a contemporary steel-and-glass world of offices and bars and computers and fax machines clearly positioned David Calder's Shylock, at least at first, as an 'insider', doing business in an office complete with glass table and computer; Shylock, though bearded, wore contemporary clothing, and clearly thought of himself as a businessman, not a Jew (Figure 2).

Though the decision to portray Shylock as, to some extent, visually similar to the Venetians, may 'solve' the moment when Portia asks 'Which is the merchant here? and which the Jew?' it of course raises a host of other questions: if Shylock seems like 'one of them' then why do the Venetians hate him so? Do they seem to the audience prejudiced rather than justifiably angry? And what about Jessica's decision to leave her father, and her religion? Does that make as much sense with an 'assimilated' Shylock? The more deeply one looks at *The Merchant of Venice*, the more difficult – and even painful – become its questions.

Simply put, the play makes people uncomfortable. Judi Dench, who played Portia at Stratford in 1971, is forthright:

> I don't think there's anything to redeem those people, I'm afraid. Everyone behaves appallingly, and there's nothing for the *spirit* in the play – which is strange for Shakespeare ... at the end of *The Merchant of Venice* I couldn't care less about anybody. As for all that about the ring at the end, I could give Portia a good slap. I wouldn't ever go to see it again.
>
> (Dench, 202, 204)

Audiences around the world have not shared Judi Dench's reaction, as is clear from the survey of notable post-war productions discussed in Samuel L. Leiter's *Shakespeare Around the Globe* (1986). But her discomfort is echoed in a thought-provoking way by John Peter, reviewing two productions of the play, at the Royal Lyceum, Edinburgh, and the Crucible, Sheffield, in 1996. 'There is nobody to like in this play, nobody to set an example; not a single character, like those sensible, worldly uncles and friends in Molière, for example, who can help you to judge anyone's merits. So whom do you praise, whom do you

FIGURE 2 In his contemporary office (anglepoise lamp, telephone and coffee mug visible), a jovial Shylock (David Calder) shakes hands with Clifford Rose's Antonio; Bassanio (Owen Teale) seems less pleased and tries to pull Antonio away. To the left, Tubal (Nick Simons), a character not normally in this scene, watches with interest. (1.3, 1993)

condemn?' (*S. Times*, 17 Nov). And the opening sentence of Jeremy Kingston's review of the 1997 Birmingham Repertory Theatre production is equally direct, 'What an odious play this is' (*Times*, 14 Feb).

Many of the questions and the uncomfortable moments in the play are Shakespeare's responsibility. But history has overtaken this play, notably the events of World War II and the Holocaust. Shakespeare wrote at a time when, as James Shapiro puts it, 'While there were not many Jews in early modern England, it was nonetheless a society surprisingly preoccupied with Jewish questions' (Shapiro, 1). Jews were expelled from England in 1290, with a decree that legalized years of mistreatment and brutality. Yet Jews, whether as whole-hearted converts to Christianity or as nominal ones (the term Marrano is sometimes used to describe those converts who secretly practised Judaism), were involved in many activities, from translating Hebrew to medicine to music. But Jews were, in some sense, like Italians, mythologized – or demonized – to serve a variety of purposes. And it is our sense of that demonization which, in the wake of the Holocaust, has made the play even more disquieting to contemporary audiences.

But to Stratford audiences such disquiet was probably much less noticeable between 1880 and 1944, when the rapid-fire Stratford schedule led to the play's appearance in thirty-seven seasons. Of course, these were not different productions but recycled ones, dominated by three major figures: Frank Benson, whose production returned for nineteen seasons from 1887 to 1916, usually with Benson playing Shylock as well as directing; William Bridges-Adams, artistic director of the Shakespeare Memorial Theatre, whose production appeared in six seasons between 1920 and 1929, and Ben Iden Payne, director of productions from 1935 through 1944, who also staged the play six times. What were these productions like? In many ways, Stratford kept alive the nineteenth-century traditions of realistically picturesque stagings, and of a reading of Shylock strongly influenced by Henry Irving's portrayal of a dignified and sympathetic, even tragic figure. Irving first produced *The Merchant of Venice* in 1879, and continued to play Shylock over a period of twenty-five years; Frank Benson had worked briefly at Irving's London base, the Lyceum, and, like Irving, became an actor–manager, though better known for touring England than for London successes (Beauman, 26–30). Given Benson's long tenure at Stratford, and the need to put together a multi-play season quickly, the productions changed very little. And although Benson's successor as artistic director, Bridges-Adams, brought to Stratford the notion of a resident, rather than a touring company, as well as a production style more influenced by Granville-Barker's continuous action than the Victorian picturesque approach, he was still hampered by insufficient funds and rehearsal time.

Still, it was Bridges-Adams who engineered Stratford's most famous pre-war production of *The Merchant of Venice* when, for the

1932 season, he invited the Russian director–designer, Theodore Komisarjevsky to Stratford – the first guest director, the first foreign director and a director willing to throw out all traditions, from realism to a 'tragic' Shylock (Bulman, 53–5). But in spite of Komisarjevsky's innovations – brightly coloured cubist-influenced sets, *commedia*-style costumes also in cheerful colours even for Antonio and Shylock, and much comic business, not only for an obvious comic such as Launcelot Gobbo, but also at the trial scene where the Duke kept falling asleep – productions that followed in the late 1930s and early 1940s were much less challenging. Under the artistic direction of Ben Iden Payne, who took over from Bridges-Adams, the stage sometimes resembled the Elizabethan stage that earlier designers (especially William Poel) had advocated, with actors in Tudor costume.

If pre-war productions at Stratford often seem to blur together – with Komisarjevsky's *The Merchant of Venice* always the exception – the thirteen productions that are the focus of this study often seem devised with 'difference' in mind. Part of each production's distinctiveness stems from the sweeping changes instituted by Barry Jackson when he took over as artistic director in 1946: young actors, many guest directors, a longer rehearsal period and plays opening on a staggered basis rather than six or eight in a two-week period. Moreover, the growing archive of production material at the Shakespeare Centre Library – books of press clippings, collections of slides and photographs and, since 1982, archival videotapes – allows directors, designers, actors to consult previous productions, to see what lines were cut from the text, to check on doubling strategies. Whether one researches past productions or not, the very existence of these archives must on some level encourage a director to try something 'new'. Further-more, the director knows that part of the audience sitting in the theatre is highly knowledgeable, composed of people who have seen the plays on a number of different occasions; such people may be theatre critics or Shakespeare scholars or Shakespeare enthusiasts who return to Stratford over and over because this is the place where the plays are done most often. Such an audience – familiar not only with the plays but with a number of interpretations of the plays – may also lure a director towards the unfamiliar, the different, frequently the shifting of period.

But, at the same time, a Stratford audience contains within it a number of people who have never seen the play before; they may, in fact, never have seen a Shakespeare play at all. Stratford-upon-Avon is, of course, a major tourist centre, and tickets to performances may come as part of a day trip, booked in advance with a travel agent. The foyer of the theatre resounds to different languages, especially in the summer. And so another pressure on the director is 'to tell the story clearly', remembering that part of the audience needs as much clarity as possible. One sign of the need to explain things to an audience which may not know the play is the 'pre-play'. Frequently directors begin the play with a kind of dumb show which immediately establishes the play's atmosphere and the relationships of the onstage characters, rather than beginning with the text's opening line which is often, as in *The Merchant of Venice*, a middle-of-the-conversation line (Smallwood, 192–3).

And, in the case of *The Merchant of Venice*, the expectations of the audience also may influence the interpretation of the play – or what the director thinks those expectations may be. With this play, an audience may already have heard of Shylock – may, in fact, think that Shylock is the merchant of Venice – and certainly may have preconceptions about the play and anti-Semitism. Here the fact of producing this play at all in the post-World War II context becomes particularly important, and anxiety-producing. A director may well know that 'letters to the editor' are waiting to be written. All of these factors will influence not only the work on the play by the director, designers and actors, but even the attempts to control the audience's response before the play has begun. Most of us consider a programme as a source of information, giving the names of the actors and photographs, as well as some background information about the play, but the programme is also, both implicitly and explicitly, a tool for manipulating the audience's reactions.

Though we think of information as 'facts' – and facts are supposed to be neutral – the information which a programme presents is far from neutral. Consider, for instance, the listing of the characters of *The Merchant of Venice*. How are characters described? Even the simple, typed sheet which was used in the 1978 production at The Other Place, listing the characters in order of speaking, includes identifying tags for each one. Only Antonio, 'a merchant of Venice', and Shylock, 'a Jew of Venice', are identified by their rank and city (as is the Duke of Venice, the only character without a tag – he exists solely through his rank); everyone else exists in relation to them. Thus, Salerio and Solanio are 'friends of Antonio and Bassanio', as is Gratiano; Lorenzo, who might also be described in this way, is, rather, 'in love with Jessica'. Bassanio gets, as it were, a double set of relationships – 'friend of Antonio, loves Portia' – while Portia is characterized only as 'in love with Bassanio'. The Prince of Morocco and the Prince of Arragon depend on Portia – 'suitor of Portia' – while Tubal, Jessica and Launcelot Gobbo are defined in relation to Shylock, friend, daughter, servant, respectively. Such descriptions subtly, but firmly, lead audiences to define characters by relationships.

In contrast, the 1960 programme (which also listed characters in order of speaking) gave Portia an identity based on place rather than on her love for Bassanio; she was 'the Lady of Belmont', the capital letters suggesting rank and power. Two previous productions (1947, 1953) emphasized her wealth, calling her 'a rich heiress'. Identifying tags for Nerissa always place her in relation to Portia, perhaps because the two women never appear separately in the play, but she can be Portia's 'maid' (1947, 1960, 1965, 1987), her 'waiting woman' (1978, 1986, 1997) or her 'friend' (1971, 1981). The first two tags sharply distinguish Nerissa's social status from that of Portia, while the third, Portia's friend, puts her on a similar social level; in 1984 and 1993 the programme simply listed

Nerissa's name, with no tag at all, identified only by being placed in the group of those at Belmont.

And, indeed, grouping the characters is another way to present them, an approach which emphasizes the difference between the play's two main worlds, Venice and Belmont. Thus, the productions of 1984, 1987 and 1993 all created two categories, Venice and Belmont. In 1984, the Venice section was subdivided so that the Duke of Venice and Antonio each occupied a separate space, followed by several groups of names; servants did not rub shoulders with noblemen, nor Christians with Jews. And in 1971, Terry Hands not only divided characters according to geography, Venice and Belmont, but then further classified the Venetians. The first subheading, 'The Merchants' (for Antonio, Salerio, Solanio and Salarino, the last-named character existing in Shakespeare's text but usually conflated with Salerio), is unexceptional. Nor is there anything particularly remarkable in calling Shylock, Tubal and Jessica 'The Jews' and Launcelot Gobbo and Old Gobbo 'The Clowns' even though we can see that each of these descriptive titles is somehow different – an occupation, a religious grouping, a dramatic convention. But the choice of 'The Venturers' for Bassanio, Gratiano and Lorenzo makes a deliberate thematic statement. We realize that there is no clear way of identifying Bassanio, Gratiano and Lorenzo by occupation or rank (though Bassanio is sometimes called 'my Lord Bassanio'); perhaps they have none, perhaps they are simply young men about town. Critics have often accused Bassanio of being a fortune-hunter, and Jessica's wealth certainly seems important to Lorenzo. The 1971 programme includes a background article entitled 'venturers' and though part of the article makes clear that 'venturing' was essentially a mercantile gamble, something we might associate more directly with Antonio than with Bassanio, the second half of the article transforms the concept into a moral good through the words of John Russell Brown: 'So the willing, generous, and prosperous transactions of love's wealth are compared and contrasted with Shylock's wholly commercial transactions in which gain is the object, enforcement the method, and even human beings are merely things to be possessed'.[1] Thus, to see Bassanio as a 'venturer' is to enhance his right to become Portia's husband. And by heading the 'venturing' page with a slight misquotation from *Romeo and Juliet*, 'wert thou as far / As that vast shore wash'd with the farthest sea / I should venture [the text reads 'adventure'] for such merchandise' (2.2.82–4), the programme-compiler leads the reader to associate the Romeo and Juliet of the balcony scene with Bassanio and Portia.

While the manipulation provided by the cast list may seem invisible, the rest of the programme is often more explicit, as the quotation from John Russell Brown in 1971 implies. And the central task of the programme-compiler, whether acknowledged or not, is to guide the audience's response, particularly to Shylock. Even the brief comments in 1960 are instructive, as the writer struggles with the conflicts created by two major characters in that season's plays: 'the villain, Shylock, and the gull, Malvolio, win our compassion'. Such a comment manages first to label Shylock and then to imply the 'correct' response to him.

Dealing with Shylock can take many forms. One tactic is to 'place' him within a Renaissance context – and that context often includes an article on 'usury', defining the practice through quotations pre-dating and contemporary with the play, as well as from more modern perspectives. The unspoken strategy might be paraphrased as 'Shakespeare isn't attacking Shylock by calling him a usurer since the period saw usury as evil'. Thus a quotation from Sir Thomas Wilson's *A Discourse on Usury* (1572) – 'that ugly, detestable and hurtful sin of USURY' – dominates a two-page spread in 1965, almost a banner headline. The text below the headline is more judicious, pointing out the contradictions – 'English law declared usury to be sinful; but all the same allowed up to 10 per cent interest on loans. Usury was tolerated with distaste; the usurer was reviled' – but the design and the selection of all the anti-usury quotations from Aristotle, from Deuteronomy, from Dante, even from Ezra Pound, support Wilson's attack.

The 1971 programme, using many of the same quotations, nonetheless produces a more balanced feel. The headline for the page is 'usury' printed twice, with one a mirror image (i.e. reversed) of the other. To the left of the headline appears a quotation from Benvenuto da Imola, 'He who practiseth usury goeth to hell, and he who practiseth it not tendeth to destitution', a statement which combines the theological with the practical. Balancing it as a headline quotation is Portia's line, 'Since you are dear bought, I will love you dear' (3.3.312), thus suggesting that mercantile considerations are as pervasive in Belmont as in Venice, and bringing together the worlds of love and money through the pun on 'dear'. The two illustrations work in the same way; on the left-hand page, we see a detail from a painting by the Flemish painter, Quentin Massys, the hands of a money-lender weighing out coins; on the right-hand page, a lover holds the hand of his lady, and the illustration is taken from the famous medieval story of love and pursuit, the *Romance of the Rose*. A similar yoking of the two worlds of the play appears on the cover of the programme for the 1986 touring production. Underneath the title of the play is the word 'contract' and the definitions that follow are 'an agreement on fixed terms, or the writing containing it, a bond' and 'a betrothal or marriage', plus its use as a verb, 'to incur (– a debt); to form (– a habit); to betroth, pledge one's faith'. The play's crucial word, 'bond', and its use in a legal context and within the marriage context, are thus swiftly and deftly joined.

This approach to Shylock-as-usurer backfired spectacularly in 1984 when many of the same quotations about usury appeared again within the context of hatred of the Jews – and hatred that appeared justifiable. Less than two weeks after the play's first preview, William Frankel wrote an angry commentary for the *Times* (17 Apr). Reacting perhaps as much to Ian McDiarmid's performance of Shylock as to the programme notes, Frankel called McDiarmid's Shylock 'comic, villainous and avaricious, cruel and insolent in success, servile in defeat', and also pointed out that the 'reproduction, in this real world, of ancient stereotypes should take into account their potential for inciting or reinforcing racial or religious prejudice'. As a result of Frankel's attack, the RSC added an introductory comment to the first page of the programme material explicitly labelling the quotations as 'offensive religious attitudes of Christian Elizabethan England' and indicating that they were designed 'to reflect the ignorance, prejudice and cruelty of the prevailing opinion in Shakespeare's day'. The programme further contextualized the material on usury by adding a paragraph which made clear (1) that Christians did lend money at interest, with the normal rate being 10 per cent and (2) that Jews could charge a higher rate because they would not be breaking Christian law and (3) that Antonio seems to be borrowing money from Shylock because 'the upstanding members of the Christian community were either not willing or not able to lend to their friend' for friendship's sake.

But the changes went much further. Particularly virulent quotations, such as the description of Jews striking and spitting at Jesus (taken from a fifteenth-century *Vie de Jesus Christ*), were reduced to smaller type. An entire page of Martin Luther's writing, including his comment, 'A Jew, a Jewish heart, are hard as wood, as stone, as iron, as the Devil himself', disappeared. So too did the quotation at the top of a page which began, 'The Jews have been punished severely from time to time. But they do not suffer innocently; they suffer because of their wickedness, because they cheat people and ruin whole countries by their usury and secret murders, as everyone knows.' In their place the programme-compiler added a full page excerpted from the American writer Mary McCarthy's 1956 book, *Venice Observed*; the commentary points to Venetian capitalism, anti-Semitism and law, and emphasizes the ironic similarities between Venetian Christians and Venetian Jews. The revised programme still makes for uncomfortable reading, but it represents a much toned-down version of what had originally – and perhaps thoughtlessly – appeared.

Yet another approach to dealing with Shylock is to admit, very openly, how difficult the problems are, rather than seeking refuge in historical context. Such was the choice of Clifford Williams in 1965, who found himself proposing that a director needs to 'wipe the slate clean and start as with a new play' and, at the same time, admitting that such a clean slate was extraordinarily difficult if one was directing, as he was, both Marlowe's *The Jew of Malta* and *The Merchant of Venice* in the same season – and, one might add, with the same actor, Eric Porter, playing Barabas and Shylock. Williams's short essay, 'Innocence and *The Merchant of Venice*', resounds with plaintive honesty. He understands – and seems to sympathize with – the argument 'that in our racist-minded age, it would be better not to stage this play at all'. He does not shy away from the ugly facts: 'Our eyes, ears and nerves will tell us that Shylock – whatever his motives and pathology – is a potential murderer, a man who *means to cut a pound of flesh from Antonio's chest*. And Shylock is a Jew!' Williams never really escapes from the trap he sees so clearly, and his discomfort is palpable. Quotations in the programme, some under the heading 'Bonds of Flesh' and others under the heading 'Children of Israel', offer both attack and defence, with the latter section pointing out the historical victimization of the Jew, from the Middle Ages through to the Third Reich.

Sometimes the choice is simply to print objections to the play, as in 1981 when John Barton directed it on the main stage, having done a production in 1978 in The Other Place. In the interim, BBC television had also broadcast its production in the series *The Shakespeare Plays*, and both in Britain and the United States, the play attracted the perhaps inevitable criticism. Marcus Shloimovitz, writing in the *Jewish Telegraph*, called the BBC production 'the finest tonic for antisemitism that the National Front or any other anti-Jewish organization could wish for', and then wrote to John Barton suggesting that the play should not be done in the 1981 Stratford season. Barton's response was to print both Shloimovitz's article and his letter, as well as a series of other comments going back to 1957, including a piece from the *Jerusalem Post* of 8 August 1980 which, though entitled 'Shylock the Loser', presents the play as balanced, with Antonio a 'noble Christian, honest in business, a generous and devoted friend', but also a man whose nobility 'stops ... at the person of Shylock'. Barton also printed his response to Shloimovitz, indicating that he did not see the play as anti-Semitic, but 'about true and false value' – and that while he respected Shloimovitz's opinion, he saw no chance that such a 'great play' would ever be withdrawn from performance.

By foregrounding the question of anti-Semitism rather than ignoring it, or allowing it to emerge from quoted material, both the 1965 and the 1981 productions also defused the kind of criticism which assailed the 1984 programme; no one could say that these directors were unaware of the emotions the play has stirred. Similarly, the 1987 production put the problem where it couldn't be missed – on the cover of the souvenir programme. The background is muted grey, the title in shaded letters so one's eye goes immediately to the gold cross and the mosaic Mogen David, also in gold, at the bottom; the cross, though small, stands over one of the points of the star, its lines vertical while the star seems flat, trampled on. Inside, the main essay is entitled 'Jews in Venice', and offers an analysis of the complex cultural and financial differences between Levantine, German and 'Western' Jews living in Venice, as well as a variety of comments from 1554 to 1975 on how Christians perceived Jews and vice versa. The second major article, 'Justice', discusses the Venetian legal system, and then moves to two pages of comments about justice and mercy, again quoting from works over a wide spectrum: ancient Roman commentary, seventeenth-century perspectives, contemporary legal scholars. The effect is to force the attentive reader to take the religious and cultural problems seriously, to see the questions as complex and compelling.

And even when questions of religion, prejudice, justice and finance are not put in a historical context, they still dominate the programme material. The 1993 production was defiantly up-to-date, from its steel-and-glass set to its loud rock music. The programme's cover, hot red-pink with bright gold Euro-coins (specially minted, I discovered, so that they could be photographed), almost throws money in the reader's face. So too does the headline, 'Money and Friendship', for two pages of quotations; so also does the essay, 'The City', commissioned for this programme from Justin Cartwright, beginning with the word 'Transactions' and exploring the idea that 'cities are markets'. In every quotation, certain words are emphasized by being set in larger type, so that particular attitudes and values leap out even at a reader who might only be browsing. Thus, the familiar quotation from Thomas Wilson about usury, appearing under a half-page spread of the coins, blown up to look like heavy dinner plates in an uneven stack, takes on a somewhat different feel, because the eye immediately sees 'ugly', 'foul', 'dealing' and 'greedy'. One may not even read the rest of the quotation or know that it is about usury, but the linking of greed and money is obvious.

So dominant is Shylock as a character – and so difficult are the questions raised by his existence both as a dramatic character and as a representative of a whole group of people – that he tends to dominate the programme too. The double-page spread of photographs from previous productions that is a regular feature of RSC programmes offers us illuminating evidence. In 1965, there is just one page of archive photographs, but they are all of famous Shylocks – Edmund Kean, Henry Irving, Beerbohm Tree, Frederick Valk, Robert Helpmann, John Gielgud, Michael Redgrave, Peter O'Toole. On the facing page, a reproduction of Charles Macklin as Shylock in the trial scene, knife and scales in hand, does also include Portia in full judicial robes and wig, but otherwise she is absent. In 1984, Portia appears more often – once on her own (from 1904), once with Bassanio (although with Shylock in the background – an obvious 'studio' photograph since no such scene appears in the play) and otherwise always in disguise as the lawyer confronting Shylock. Of the fourteen photographs, thirteen give us Shylock or Shylock and Portia. In 1987, there are fourteen photographs with Shylock in every one – and in seven of them, he is alone. Otherwise we see him with Antonio (twice), with Portia in disguise (four times) and, surprisingly, with Jessica. And in 1993, the eleven archival photographs concentrate again on Shylock – one is of Peggy Ashcroft as the disguised Portia, and all the others show us Shylock, alone, or with Portia as the lawyer, or with Antonio.

Occasionally the photographs offer a more balanced view. In 1971, they begin with a page of two rehearsal photographs – on top, Bassanio and Portia, scripts in hand (Michael Williams and Judi Dench), below a close-up of Emrys James (Shylock). And the archival photographs are similarly balanced – a page for Shylock (seven photographs) and on the facing page five different Bassanios and Portias. As always the contrast is not just between characters, but between recurring motifs. Shylock is almost always bearded, usually pictured in brooding close-up, while Portia and Bassanio gaze into each other's eyes – isolation vs. love. In 1981, the cover photograph is, remarkably, of Portia (Sinead Cusack). Here *she* is the brooding figure, her arms crossed over her chest, her sad eyes staring at three small caskets. And inside the programme, the visual emphasis on Portia continues: she and Bassanio (Jonathan Hyde) in rehearsal clothes frame Anne Barton's essay on the play, their hands meeting in the middle of the two-page spread as Portia gives Bassanio the ring. The archive photographs are not separated as they are in 1971; instead, there are seven of Bassanio and Portia, interspersed with six of Shylock on his own, one of Portia by herself and one of Portia and Shylock. And in 1997, when again, unusually, the programme cover focuses on the casket story (with three figures, in gold, silver and lead), the photographs show us almost everyone in the cast; Bassanio appears in four photographs, Portia in four and Shylock only in three. The play, as represented by these three programmes, is as much about Portia and Bassanio as it is about Shylock, but the choice is an unusual one for programme-compilers to make. More usually, the photographs tell us – and particularly they tell someone who does not know the play – the same story; this is a play about a bearded man with scales, or with a legal document, or, more often, with a knife. This play, the programmes tell us, over and over, is about Shylock.

What the photographs also tell us is how much the look of the play keeps changing. The thirteen productions of *The Merchant of Venice* studied here are set in a wide variety of periods and present often highly contrasting approaches to the central characters and their relationships, although usually within a context of psychological realism and a clearly identifiable social world. Despite the iconoclasm of Komisarjevsky – or perhaps because that 1932 production was so unusual – no director at Stratford has since tried as deliberately as he did for broad comedy or stylized costumes. Instead, starting with Michael Benthall's 1947 production, featuring John Ruddock as Shylock and Beatrix Lehmann as Portia, the major design choice was to set the play in the Italian Renaissance, although a Renaissance suggested primarily by gorgeous costumes and, often, many supernumeraries. Benthall used thirty-one actors for a production referred to as 'decorative' (*Times*). Denis Carey, directing the play in 1953, used forty-two actors, led by Michael Redgrave's Shylock and Peggy Ashcroft's Portia; a unit set with a variety of levels served both Venice and Belmont. In 1956, Margaret Webster, the only woman (and the only American) to direct the play at Stratford, created a series of beautiful pictures with shimmering costumes for Belmont and Alan Tagg's lightly graceful sets for Venice; like Benthall and Carey, she filled the stages with supernumeraries (thirty-eight in the company), and continued to present a shabby, even greasy, Shylock (Emlyn Williams) as opposed to a fairy-tale Portia (Margaret Johnston).

The first move away from the Italian Renaissance came in 1960 when Michael Langham directed Peter O'Toole (Shylock) and Dorothy Tutin (Portia) in a production set in the eighteenth century. Dominated by the young O'Toole (who was twenty-eight years old) in a fierce and virile performance, this production included a number of actors (out of a company of thirty-seven) who were to appear in the play again in larger roles: Tony Church (the Duke) would become Antonio in 1971 as would Clifford Rose (Stephano) in 1993; Philip Voss would rise from Morocco's servant and the Officer of the Court to Shylock (1997). And Ian Richardson (Arragon), Ian Holm (Lorenzo), Roy Dotrice (a servant) and Diana Rigg (casket-polisher) would all become familiar figures in Stratford and London. The last production on this scale (thirty-six actors) was the 1965 production directed by Clifford Williams. Again the setting was Renaissance, and the production played in repertory with Marlowe's *The Jew of Malta*, the other major English Renaissance play to feature a Jew as the central character; Eric Porter played both Shylock and Barabas, with Janet Suzman as Portia.

The lavishness of these five productions – especially when one considers the number of actors and costumes used – stands in sharp contrast to the productions from 1971 on. Terry Hands used just twenty actors, led by Emrys James (Shylock) and Judi Dench (Portia); the brown-box unit set was the same for Venice and Belmont, although Belmont was dominated by caskets so large and so sculpted that one immediately thought of the funeral connotation for a casket. And when John Barton directed the play in 1978 at The Other Place, the stripped-down approach continued: fifteen actors (with, of course, some doubling), a park bench and small table for Belmont, a café table and a few chairs for Venice, and the cast in nineteenth-century costume. Patrick Stewart was the tough and unsentimental Shylock, Marjorie Bland the trapped Portia. Three years later, in 1981, Barton directed the play again, this time in Stratford's main house, with David Suchet as Shylock and Sinead Cusack as Portia. With Christopher Morley again the designer, the production looked very much the same, but Suchet's 'laughing Shylock' gave the play a very different tone. Once the nineteenth-century setting became familiar, as a result of Barton's work, productions at Stratford tended to move back and forth between Renaissance settings and costumes on the one hand, and either nineteenth- or twentieth-century settings on the other. The sumptuously dressed – and to many eyes, overdressed – John Caird production of 1984 (designed by Ultz) featured a stage draped with deep rich red figured tapestries; the Venetian nobles wore brightly coloured costumes (not Antonio, of course), and Portia (Frances Tomelty) was resplendent in a bright-blue satin dress. Ian McDiarmid's black-clad Shylock was a fiercely dominating figure, even with a tall, yellow pointed hat as the most visible sign of his outsider status. In contrast, the 1986 touring production, directed by Roger Michell, with Nigel Terry as Shylock and Fiona Shaw as Portia, moved again to the nineteenth century, this time with a frock coat for Terry's youngish Shylock, and a similar costume for Shaw when she appeared in court.

The last three productions of the century continued the alternating pattern, with a return to the Italian Renaissance in Bill Alexander's 1987 production. But the main-stage set was much more sombre than previous Renaissance productions. The wooden planks and bridge suggested a lonely rather than a lovely Venice. The back wall of the theatre, all in brick, carried two conflicting religious emblems, a golden icon in Byzantine style of the Virgin, and a scrawled yellow Mogen David. Antony Sher's Shylock was a cultural as well as religious outsider, clearly a figure from the Middle East, living in the shadows, while Deborah Findlay's Portia, dressed in lavish and decorative fashion, had tidy little caskets shaped like small houses and met her suitors in bright light. For his 1993 production, David Thacker moved both Venice and Belmont into the late twentieth century, with Venice as the financial capital (filled with up-to-date office machinery) and Belmont as a stylized mansion with sleekly elegant stands for the small caskets, but no other furniture. David Calder's Shylock began as a comfortable, affable financier and ended as an embittered outsider, while Penny Downie's Portia, first seen in a black evening dress, became an increasingly commanding figure, especially in the trial scene in her spectacles and severe suit. And in 1997, Venice and Belmont returned to the Renaissance, with a dark and shadowy Venice and a tall narrow house for Philip Voss's

Shylock, and a golden arch which flew in for the Belmont of Helen Schlesinger's Portia. Gregory Doran, who played Solanio in 1987, directed the production.

My study of these productions derives from several sources. I have personally seen seven productions (1971, 1978, 1981, 1984, 1987, 1993, 1997) and have drawn on my notes from those viewings, as well as conversations with several of the actors and essays from the series *Players of Shakespeare*. The central resources lie in the Shakespeare Centre Library, where I have consulted the promptbooks, programmes, reviews and photographs for all thirteen of the productions. In some cases, a single phrase from a review offers a significant detail, but archival videotapes (available from 1981 on) have helped to fill in gaps, and the production records, comprising cast lists, costume charts, rehearsal calls, prop lists, stage-manager reports, and occasionally the deputy stage manager's rehearsal notes, have also been extremely helpful. Inevitably, some productions get more attention than others, not just because I have seen them, but because they present more interesting, and often more disturbing, views of the play than others. For this study is not a chronological or full account of thirteen productions, but rather an analysis of how Stratford productions since 1945 have reshaped and reinterpreted the play.

One non-Stratford production deserves special mention since it seems to me a ground-breaking interpretation in a number of ways. When Jonathan Miller directed the play with Laurence Olivier as Shylock in 1970 (National Theatre, London), he set the play in 1880 with outdoor scenes evoking a café society and indoor scenes filled with elaborate props, thus creating a world of real businessmen and wealthy women. The trial scene, tellingly, took place around a table rather than in a large public courtroom, since, as Miller later wrote, 'This dispute was too ugly to be argued out in public. The courtroom disappeared and was replaced in my mind by a rather drab Justice's Chambers' (Miller, 107). Such a scaling down extended to Olivier himself who had first planned Shylock as a 'grotesque, ornamentally Jewish figure' but who gradually came to look 'much more like everybody else' (107). From the decisions about set to the resulting decisions about character, Miller's production moved the play into contexts not just of modern anti-Semitism, politely disguised, but of homo-social relationships, also politely disguised. But, given that the director of the National Theatre and one of England's greatest actors (Olivier became the first theatrical lord during the run of this production) was playing Shylock, this production continued to emphasize Shylock's centrality. The nineteenth-century setting, the problematic relationship between Antonio and Bassanio, the implicit (and sometimes explicit) criticism of both Belmont and Venice, and the continuing power of Shylock – all captured on videotape as well as on stage – make Miller's production one that haunts the imagination still.

Our look at RSC productions will begin with Shylock, the first scenes in which he appears and the question of his status in Venice. Since the portrayal of Shylock is inextricably bound up with the representation of Venice, I look next at the Venetian opposition to Shylock, first the gentlemen who find themselves needing the man they despise, and then his servant, Launcelot Gobbo. While the play's other world, Belmont, seems different from the almost exclusively male-dominated and mercantile Venice, it nonetheless has its problematic aspects, as chapter 4 indicates. We then return to Venice, for another look at Shylock, focusing first on his reaction to the loss of his daughter, and the money she has taken with her, and then on the play's great fourth act, where all the major characters confront each other. The final chapter revisits Belmont, asking, as the play does, what kinds of reconciliation are possible for couples whose unions have been threatened, not just by Shylock but by their own broken promises.

NOTE

1 The quotation is taken from John Russell Brown's *Shakespeare and His Comedies* (London, 1957), 67.

1

SHYLOCK

As the Introduction suggests, many of the questions which first strike an audience of the play centre on the figure of Shylock. It may therefore come as a shock to note that Shylock 'appears in only five scenes and two of these are very brief' (Stewart, 13). Still, the role is the second longest in the play – only Portia has more lines. And whenever Shylock does appear, he is the centre of attention; even when he is not on stage, people are talking about him. Only in Belmont, during the scenes with Portia and her first two wooers, is he absent. But once he has appeared in Venice, he is, whether on stage or not, the controlling force of the play. Launcelot Gobbo debates with himself about whether or not to leave Shylock's service; the elopement of Jessica with Lorenzo reminds us of the suffocating power that Shylock seems to possess; after the elopement, we do not see Shylock himself, but Salerio and Solanio vividly – and maliciously – imitate his shock on finding that he has lost both daughter and treasure; and after Bassanio chooses the right casket and thus wins Portia's hand, the arrival of Salerio from Venice, together with Lorenzo and Jessica, brings Shylock and his threats against Antonio right back to centre stage.

But more than the events of the plot contribute to Shylock's peculiar force. Shylock's language, rich in its allusions, full of emphatic repetition, structured by deliberately parallel constructions, moving with ease from prose to verse and back again, characterizes him with particular vividness. His opening line, 'Three thousand ducats, well' (1.3.1), immediately focuses our attention on money, and indeed on the large amount that will come to dominate the play.[1] And the monosyllable, 'Well', allows for a variety of readings: perhaps a brisk summing up of the situation, or an extended drawl as if considering just how large a sum three thousand ducats really is, or an agreement in principle if not in fact. Whatever the choice of the actor, he can immediately vary it or sustain it, since Shylock's next two lines, 'For three months, well' and 'Antonio shall become bound, well', end with the same monosyllable. Line after line characterizes the man and his many facets. Patrick Stewart reports that he was 'delighted to discover how marvellously witty Shylock was, particularly in the early part of the play' (Stewart, 14), and his perception is one shared by most Shylocks and most audiences. Shylock is quick to appropriate and reinterpret the words of others. When he insists to Antonio that he is willing to lend money without interest, 'This is kind I offer', and Bassanio hopefully chimes in, 'This were kindness', Shylock immediately recaptures the word for himself, 'This kindness will I show' (1.3.138–9).

Furthermore, Shylock controls the conversation through rhetorical delay, as we hear in his long speech about Jacob and Laban (1.3.71–85), a speech which, however obscure the story, has never in recent RSC productions been cut or even trimmed. This speech, detailing how Jacob managed to get spotted lambs from his father-in-law, is Shylock's way of making Antonio and Bassanio squirm. He knows that they want his answer about whether or not he will lend them money, and instead of giving that answer, he makes them listen to him talk about Jacob. Similarly, when Antonio asks a bit later, 'Well Shylock, shall we be beholding to you?' (100), Shylock not only makes Antonio wait, but further embarrasses him by assuming the role of a subordinate and by referring repeatedly to Antonio's epithet, 'dog'. A similar exercise of power through language occurs in 4.1 as Shylock responds to the Duke of Venice's naive and condescending speech in which the Duke tries to get Shylock to back away from his claim. Instead of giving the expected 'gentle answer' (the phrase contains, of course, a chilling pun, gentle/Gentile), Shylock takes over twenty lines to say, in effect, that he will continue his suit because he hates Antonio (43–62). The proliferation of examples designed to mock and embarrass the Venetians as well as the length of the speech lets us know that he is savouring every moment of his delay.

Thus, every actor who approaches the role of Shylock will find a vivid and highly defined character, even in speeches which may seem 'off the point'. It's worth noting that though RSC productions frequently trim lines from the play Shylock's role has been almost totally exempt from cuts. But even with such specific writing, the choices for the actor are many. And perhaps the biggest choice lies in the relationship of Shylock to the Venetian community. Simply put, is he the exotic outsider or a potential insider?

The familiar, even traditional, choice is to make Shylock a foreign, often exotic, figure. His appearance is startlingly different, whether seen as Peter O'Toole's bearded 'Christ in torment' (*E. News*) among a group of eighteenth-century aristocrats elegant in light colours and satin clothes (1960), or Antony Sher's beturbaned Levantine Jew (see cover), with long swirling robes, set against European Venetians of the Renaissance (1987). In the elaborately costumed production of 1984, with the Venetians a-glitter in brightly coloured and sequined costumes, Ian McDiarmid's dark, flowing robes, to say nothing of his tall, pointed, yellow hat, became the signs of difference. These Shylocks, though emphatically different, seemed to have moved up in class from Michael Redgrave (1953) and Emlyn Williams (1956), both of whom were compared to Dickens's master thief, Fagin. Paul Holt described Redgrave as 'Father Abraham, grey and ponderous, a bit of a Fagin, a bit of a shady car-salesman. He is greasy, hissing, hiccoughing' (*D. Herald*). Williams seemed even more repulsive, so much so that one reviewer asked plaintively, 'Why must Shylock so often look so dirty and bedraggled' (*Glos. Echo*), and the damning adjective 'greasy' reappears in Cecil Wilson's phrase, 'this grey, greasy, shambling Shylock' (*D. Mail*). Williams also wore a yellow Mogen David on his robe (partially visible in Figure 1, p. 5); in the trial scene, where it was covered by a dark cloak, he pointedly showed the sign of his difference when he spoke of his 'lodged hate' for Antonio.

Such a Shylock often sounds different too. O'Toole used a slight, but noticeable, accent; Emrys James (1971) used his own Welsh accent (as did Williams in 1956), thus supplying another version of 'outsider' to English-tuned ears; Ian McDiarmid (1984) used a pronounced Yiddish accent; and Sher (1987) similarly offered an 'exhilaratingly thickly accented, long-haired and colourfully Semitic' Shylock (*FT*). Shylock's difference has also been emphasized by the portrayal of his daughter Jessica who usually appears in costumes quite different from those worn by the other women in the play, Portia and Nerissa.

And, although the prevailing mode of set design in the second half of the century has eliminated the use of radically different sets for various locations, directors and designers have frequently isolated Shylock's space through rearrangement of set pieces and through lighting. The two huge pipe organs used throughout the 1984 production normally remained up stage, in the left and right corners, but for the scenes involving Jessica's elopement, they slid downstage to provide both a 'balcony' level from which Jessica could look out and a heavy, suffocating area from which she needed to escape. In 1987, designer Kit Surrey, working essentially with a bare wooden floor that resembled a Venetian landing stage, backed by a brick wall with both an icon of the Madonna carefully painted on it and a yellow star scrawled across it, brought in carpets, pillows and a small canopy propped up as a tent, to give Shylock a noticeably different surrounding. Indeed, the Bassanio of this production glanced around anxiously when he first spoke to Shylock, as if aware that he had somehow stumbled into a remote, even dangerous, part of town (Figure 3).

FIGURE 3 Shylock (Antony Sher) reclines on his low couch, while listening to the request of Antonio (John Carlisle, centre) and Bassanio (Nicholas Farrell). A small canopy (the pole is visible) suggests a Levantine background for Shylock, and his low table contains a balance, abacus and bell. (1.3, 1987)

Playing Shylock as an outsider reflects not only Shakespeare's text, with its emphasis on Shylock as 'Jew', rather than as individual, and Portia's ultimate weapon, the law which privileges the citizen against the 'alien', but also European Renaissance culture. By the time Shakespeare wrote his play in the last decade of the sixteenth century, Jews had been officially exiled from England for about three hundred years (Shapiro, 46–55) and from Spain for at least a hundred, even though converted Jews whose background was well known and, in some cases, Jews who practised their religion in secret are still noted in various records; indeed, as Shapiro points out, Henry VIII consulted Jewish advisors when he needed legal advice on divorcing Catherine of Aragon (Shapiro, 68). The presence of Jewish musicians from Italy at the court of Queen Elizabeth was also well known, including the Bassano family, whose name may be reflected in Bassanio; and the Queen's doctor, Roderigo Lopez, was a Portuguese Jew, whose trial and execution may be alluded to in the trial scene when Gratiano speaks of the connection between Shylock's 'currish spirit' and the 'fell soul' of the 'wolf [lupus/lopez] ... hang'd for human slaughter' (4.1.133–5).

But in Italy, and particularly in Venice, communities of Jews existed openly, though under strict constraints. Jews in Venice were economically necessary, serving as money-lenders, and legally protected as early as 1385, allowed to live in Venice and transact business on the Rialto. But they were limited in terms of occupation (in addition to lending money, they could buy and sell used clothes), they could not own land, and they were forced to wear a distinguishing badge, first a yellow circle or a yellow scarf (for men and women, respectively) and then a yellow hat. And, in 1516, Jews were formally segregated into a section of Venice which was called the *getto* or *ghetto*. The open square known as the Ghetto Nuovo was essentially an island within an island, surrounded by canals, and with only two bridges as exits. Gates at these bridges were guarded, and closed from sunset until dawn. The creation of a Jewish community, barely tolerated and forcibly isolated, has become a familiar historical entity, and its name, ghetto, probably comes from Venice. So representing Shylock as a figure from this well-known cultural identity would have made sense to Shakespeare's audience.

But alongside this well-established tradition of playing Shylock as the outsider, the RSC has also developed what one might call a parallel tradition, namely that of seeing Shylock not as an exotic alien, but as a substantial businessman who superficially resembles the Venetian citizens, and who may even think that he is 'one of them'. The National Theatre led the way with Jonathan Miller's 1970 production, and in 1978 John Barton's in The Other Place also put the play in a late nineteenth-century setting. However, unlike Olivier's dapper merchant banker (1970), or the greasy 'alien' Shylocks, Patrick Stewart's Shylock chose to wear shabby clothes because he was thrifty (or mean), just as he rolled his own cigarettes and carefully put the little unsmoked ends back in a tin for future re-use. His Jewishness was submerged, with the fringes of his prayer-shawl barely showing beneath his dark waistcoat, although, like earlier Shylocks, Stewart was bearded and wore the traditional yarmulke (Figure 4). By 1981, when Barton remounted the play on the main stage of the Royal Shakespeare Theatre, with David Suchet now playing Shylock, Shylock's wealth and assimilationist tendencies were much more visible. Suchet's Shylock wore a fur-trimmed overcoat; he smoked cigars rather than hand-rolled cigarettes; and he carried a cane. In the play's opening scene, Antonio, Salerio and Solanio were drinking brandy and smoking cigars; they too had canes, as did Bassanio, these props connoting an elegance and wealth that was associated both with the Venetians and with Shylock the Jew. The 1986 touring production directed by Roger Michell seems to have derived its Victorian look from this second Barton production, from its opening scene at a café table to its formally clad Shylock.

And in 1993, with a production set in the business world of contemporary London, both Shylock and Bassanio inhabited a world of computers and telephones. Indeed, Bassanio seemed just one of a team of stockbrokers in a large office spread out over two upper levels of a huge steel structure (see Figure 8, p. 46) while Shylock was clearly a managing director inhabiting his own spacious office on the main stage, with an elegant glass-topped table for his desk, and a laptop computer. The only overt sign of his difference was the presence of a large, leather-bound Bible on a reading stand. This production emphasized Shylock's likeness to the Venetians by dressing him in a well-cut dark suit, and by contrasting him with Tubal, a character whose first textual appearance is in 3.1, but who now appeared in 1.3 as well, Shylock's first scene (see Figure 2, p. 7). This Tubal, dressed like an Orthodox Jew, with long dark coat, yarmulke, long side curls, visibly foreign, emphasized Shylock's assimilated look. He did not speak (there are, after all, no lines for him in 1.3) but when

FIGURE 4 Furred collars are visible on the overcoats of Bassanio (John Nettles) and Antonio (David Bradley) as they confront the more shabbily dressed Shylock of Patrick Stewart. (1.3, 1978)

Shylock hesitated about lending money to Bassanio, checking his computer screen as if scanning his bank balance, Tubal came over to him, and whispered in his ear, thus prompting Shylock's line, 'Tubal (a wealthy Hebrew of my tribe) / Will furnish me' (52–3).

These four productions were set either in the late nineteenth century or (1993) in the twentieth century, and it is difficult to know whether the setting has created the 'new' approach to Shylock, or whether the approach to Shylock has influenced the setting. Certainly the official attitude to Jews in England has seen enormous changes since Shakespeare's time. Cromwell's government debated the readmission of Jews to England at the Whitehall Conference of 1655, although, as Shapiro points out, there were already Jews living in England, despite the 'expulsion' of 1290. Jews became both more numerous and more prominent in English life during the seventeenth and eighteenth centuries. The Jewish Naturalization Act (or 'Jew Bill'), allowing Jews to be naturalized without taking the Holy Sacrament, was passed in the spring of 1753 and then repealed in November of the same year, a turnaround which reveals the deep rifts, both religious and political, in English attitudes towards any non-conforming strangers. But, by the middle of the nineteenth century, much had changed. Benjamin Disraeli was elected to Parliament in 1837, became leader of the Conservative Party in 1848 and served twice as Prime Minister, briefly in 1868 and then from 1874 to 1880. And though no other Jew in England achieved such high political office, the name of the Rothschild family of bankers became almost synonymous with great wealth.

Thus, any production set in the nineteenth century or later would, almost inevitably, have to take into account the socially much more accepted figure of the Jew. And there is even textual justification for seeing Shylock as 'one among many businessmen, scarcely distinguishable from them' (Miller, 155). Shylock's most famous speech insists on the likeness between Jews and others, not on their difference, and Miller's production, with Olivier's Shylock clean-shaven, dressed in frock coat and top hat, showed how the superficial visual similarity highlighted the very deep prejudice which still existed.

Though Miller's production brought the nineteenth-century setting and the possible likeness of Shylock and Antonio to the fore, the RSC would, I think, have eventually tried out a nineteenth-century *Merchant*, in large part because the period allows a director to convey detailed personal and social relation-ships. John Barton recognized that quality when he talked about Shakespeare's other 'Venetian' play, *Othello*, to Julia Trevelyan Oman who would design his 1971 production of the tragedy (and who had the previous year designed Miller's *The Merchant of Venice*):

> I wanted a world of workaday soldiers, unglamorous, with Iago the norm, and Othello standing out as a romantic figure ... The more workaday the norm of the play was, the more it helps to set off

Othello as an exotic figure. Again, if it's Renaissance, Othello has no
particular extraordinariness, because we haven't got a social sense
about the Renaissance.   (Greenwald, 138)

Ralph Berry offers an even more useful rationale when he calls the
nineteenth century 'the most vivid of all preceding centuries to
us, and the most apt for exploitation' precisely because it is 'the
great age of property. Property means props: you can illustrate
great wealth, or bourgeois comfort, in a way that is impossible
before or since' (Berry, 172–3). And since Barton's 1978 *Merchant*
was staged in The Other Place, the small black-box theatre in
which sets are usually minimal, a period setting which would
define characters by costumes and hand-props might seem even
more inviting. The scaled-down budgets for productions at The
Other Place meant that elaborate costumes and scenery simply
were not possible; indeed, the record of negotiations for the
garden bench which formed the main piece of furniture at
Belmont in 1978 shows that the theatre planned to borrow a
bench rather than buy it.

Though the experimentation with period and setting for *The
Merchant of Venice* began in The Other Place, the main stage soon
featured a similar approach, when Barton restaged his 1978
production in 1981. Both of these productions, as well as the
ultra-modern 1993 production, raised questions about our understanding of Shylock, his social position and the hatred felt towards
him. Patrick Stewart's Shylock was, as I've suggested, defined more
by class than by religion; his shabbiness set him apart, made him
someone more easily despised. David Suchet's Shylock was,
visually, much more like the Venetians, and his affable, humorous
manner, his speech often interspersed with laughter, made him
easier for the Venetians to deal with; Irving Wardle called him 'the
laughing Shylock' (*Times*). Yet both Stewart and Suchet never
forgot that they were aliens, and neither could be totally surprised
by the reversal in the trial scene. However, in 1993, David Calder's
Shylock showed a man initially less aware of his Jewishness, who

later embraced his religious and cultural identity deliberately. As Calder said, in conversation with me, Shylock not only thinks he can operate easily within the system, but doesn't really see that there is a problem. Calder's Shylock knew that Antonio hated him and was ironically aware of Antonio's condescension (he laughed when Antonio said 'gentle Jew', 1.3.173, and then threw the audience a look as if to say, 'well, I have to put up with these terrible gentle/gentile puns, don't I?') but figured that they could still do business. So, for Calder, the betrayal by Jessica – her leaving, and with a Christian – was not only unexpected, but shattering. And when he reappeared in 3.1, he resembled Tubal, wearing a long dark coat rather than his smart jacket, his shirt open to reveal a Mogen David around his neck. Talking to Tubal, he stressed the emotional loss rather than the financial loss; dropped were the lines 'a diamond gone cost me two thousand ducats in Frankfurt ... two thousand ducats in that, and other precious, precious jewels' (76–7, 79–80) and 'I know not what's spent in the search' (83–4). Instead Calder gave heartfelt stress to 'the curse never fell upon my [the text reads 'our'] nation till now, I never felt it till now' (77–9). What happened to the assimilated Shylock in the 1993 production was that he became a Jew by virtue of being persecuted for being a Jew. The man who thought he could do business with the Christians, and not only survive but prosper, discovered that he must, after all, accept his alien status. By the time he appeared in the courtroom, Shylock replaced Tubal visually as the alien Jew.

Interestingly enough, Jessica, Shylock's daughter, has in production continued to remain an 'alien' figure, no matter whether her father is visually a stranger or not. In productions with an 'alien' Shylock, such a presentation seems only logical. But it's perhaps surprising to find that even when Shylock seemed to blend into the Venetian world, Jessica did not. Avril Carson, Jessica to Patrick Stewart's Shylock (1978), wore a black caftan, its loose flowing lines and Arabic-looking embroidery a clear contrast to the tightly fitted black dress of Marjorie Bland's Portia. Judy

Buxton, Jessica to David Suchet's Shylock (1981), was an even more striking contrast; first seen in a shapeless black dress covered with an apron, her hair bound up in a kerchief, she looked like a domestic servant rather than the daughter of an obviously wealthy man (Figure 5). Her accent, like Shylock's, set her apart, and not until the last act, when she wore a white dress, did she seem to fit into the new world she had joined. Rachel Joyce, playing Jessica in the 1986 touring production, looked more like an office assistant to her father, with a tight black-velvet jacket, trimmed with white collar and white cuffs over a flowered skirt; given the economics of touring, she signalled her 'change' by simply taking off the jacket, revealing a scoop neck to the flowered dress, and, in the final scene, releasing her long hair from the more formal, swept-back style of earlier scenes. In a sense, she anticipated the most emancipated Jessica, that of Kate Duchêne, in the 1993 production. Here it was clear that Jessica, efficient in her blue suit, was the administrative assistant to David Calder's Shylock. Unlike other Jessicas who were always confined to Shylock's house, she first appeared in Shylock's office; such a choice would, of course, make sense of the possibility of meeting Lorenzo, one of the group of young men working in the 'offices' upstairs. But it was more difficult to see what she was escaping from, whereas Buxton's Jessica clearly was trapped in a life of drudgery and repression. Only the sober colour of Duchêne's blue suit, unenlivened by scarf or jewellery, suggested just how limited her existence might really be.

For how one sees Jessica – and her relationship to Shylock – has become more and more an index to understanding Shylock himself, whether that understanding leads the audience to feel more sympathy for him, or to see him as an unpleasantly repressive father. The short scene between Shylock and Jessica (2.5) is crucial here, and the promptbook texts are remarkably consistent in keeping the scene pretty much intact. In 1987, perhaps in an attempt to lessen the old stereotype of the Jew as miser, Shylock's line, 'For I did dream of money-bags to-night' (18),

FIGURE 5 Shylock (David Suchet) possessively holds on to Jessica's hand as he reacts with angry suspicion to Launcelot Gobbo (Rob Edwards). Shylock wears a richly patterned dressing gown and holds a cigar, but Jessica (Judy Buxton), in dark dress and kerchief covering her hair, seems more like a household servant. (2.5, 1981)

disappeared, and occasionally some of Launcelot Gobbo's nonsense, as he tries to cover up his mention of a 'masque', a word that lights Shylock's anger, and perhaps even his suspicion, has been cut. More often, there have been interpolations, with Shylock calling more insistently for Jessica, as John Ruddock (1947) and Emrys James (1971) did, with an extra 'What Jessica' at the beginning of the scene; indeed, in 1971 (and again in 1981), the previous scene with Jessica, 2.3, had ended with an offstage (and non-textual) call of 'Jessica' from Shylock, a call which suggests that he is constantly checking up on her.

Patrick Stewart has called 2.5 'Shylock's most private scene', one in which 'there is no need for a public face and the unrestrained man will emerge' (Stewart, 21), and productions have revealed radically different views of that private man. Stewart's Shylock essentially reflected the view put forth by both Launcelot Gobbo and Jessica, the servant speaking of Shylock as 'a kind of devil' (2.2.23), the daughter saying 'Our house is hell' (2.3.2). As Stewart wrote, 'It is not the hell of poverty or meanness or even cruelty, but the hell of a house from which love has been withdrawn' (Stewart, 22). After letting Jessica brush his coat (or perhaps implicitly forcing her to do so), and after locking up the money he has been weighing in his desk, he crossed to Jessica with the line, 'Well Jessica go in' (2.5.50), and then, holding her chin and staring at her, suddenly, without warning, slapped her across the face. Stewart had an explanation: 'Perhaps Shylock sees in Jessica's eyes something of her inexplicable defiance and her intended escape. I saw it and struck at her face in anger and frustration – painful and humiliating for her and for Shylock' (Stewart, 22). But no one who saw the production can forget the surprise and shock of the moment; Roger Warren spoke of the 'quite gratuitous slap in the face' (SS, 204), and Ann Jennalie Cook called it 'shocking, gratuitous cruelty' (SQ, 159). Jessica has, at least in Shylock's presence, done nothing – yet – to deserve such treatment. Shylock's departure was then followed by the only response possible, as Jessica crossed to the desk, used the keys he had given her to unlock it and took out a bag of money.

But other Jessicas and other Shylocks have found relationships which allow for the possibility of genuine affection between father and daughter. Peter O'Toole's Shylock, in 1960, kissed Jessica before he left the house. Ian McDiarmid, in 1984, gave Jessica an ear-ring and a ring, kissed her when he said, 'Well Jessica go in', then gave her another ring, this one the turquoise that he will later identify as his late wife's gift to him, and hugged her once more. Perhaps he was just giving her the jewellery for safe keeping, but it was noticeable that he gave the jewels to her rather than locking them away. So too did Antony Sher's Shylock hand over a ring to Deborah Goodman's Jessica, kissing it before he put it on her finger (1987); she then kissed the ring, suggesting that this was a familiar ritual, the ring a symbol of the woman they both loved. And here too there were father/daughter embraces, though more formal ones: Jessica kissed Shylock's hand, he kissed her forehead before leaving. Once he was gone, Jessica made clear where her affections would henceforth be, as she took out the crucifix on a chain which Launcelot Gobbo had given to her, and which he had received from her lover, Lorenzo. Her final couplet became a complex pun, 'Farewell, – and if my fortune be not crost, / I have a father, you a daughter, lost' (2.5.55-6). Her fortune was to be with the cross, with the Christian community, or at least she hoped so.

How an audience feels about Jessica and especially the extent to which it sympathizes with her elopement may well colour its view of Shylock. For if Shylock's house truly is 'hell', then her escape not only makes sense but seems desirable. To leave a father who, like Patrick Stewart's Shylock, slapped his daughter seems a form of self-preservation rather than rebellion; to leave a Shylock as foreign as Antony Sher, one who was openly mocked and spat upon by Venetians, and outside whose 'house' a trio of street urchins (known in the promptbook as 'freaks') made mocking noises and even echoed the call 'Why Jessica' also seems plausible. Early in the rehearsal process, the director even imagined the possibility of a dramatic escape for Jessica, using knotted sheets and climbing down the proscenium arch; safety considerations, as well as Jessica's possession of the keys, led to a more conventional exit, but the idea was clearly to emphasize her desperate need to get away from Shylock. Judy Buxton, Jessica in 1981, has spoken to me of feeling 'smothered', and that word offers yet another approach to the Shylock/Jessica relationship. David Suchet's Shylock hugged and kissed her, offering the possibility that Jessica might be fleeing an over-demonstrative father. That interpretation was even more visible in 1997, with Philip Voss's Shylock a man who constantly stood too close to people, 'invading their space', and who certainly touched Jessica (Emma Handy) frequently during 2.5. And since all of these Jessicas were leaving environments which seemed either foreign or businesslike, one could understand the wish for a different place; indeed, Handy's Jessica escaped from a dark and narrow house, its high stone walls visually imprisoning her.

But leaving a rather warm and cosy environment, such as surrounded David Calder's Shylock in this scene, was much more difficult. Whereas other 'modern-dress' productions suggested that Shylock's home was still essentially his office, especially the 1978 and 1981 productions which showed Shylock weighing out money while calling for Jessica, the 1993 production clearly distinguished workplace and home. At home, Shylock appeared in a smoking jacket, turned on a stereo player to listen to Brahms, crossed to a table, lighted a candle, picked up a framed photograph and even blew a speck of dust off it, and then sat down in an armchair, looking at the photograph (of, we assumed, his wife), and was lost in thought when Launcelot Gobbo appeared. Such actions and the setting gave us a gentle, cultured Shylock, even a considerate one who, though warning Launcelot Gobbo that there would be less food available at Bassanio's, still had a letter ready to hand over to him; the promptbook called it a 'reference', but it could equally have been a parting cheque. The music from the stereo didn't last for the entire scene; indeed, once Shylock heard about the street masques, he switched off the stereo. And Jessica had obviously heard his comments about popular music before, since she crossed away from her father and curled up in the armchair, as if protecting herself from an over-familiar lecture (Figure 6). But despite her resistance to her father, one saw her inner conflict; she helped Shylock put on his coat and scarf, she received his kiss, and then, after he started to leave, she suddenly kissed him. His surprised look indicated that this was an unexpected, even unusual, gesture from her. It suggested that, although her mind was made up to leave her father, she still had feelings for him, still worried about what she was doing. Shylock's line, 'Perhaps I will return immediately', seemed prompted by that kiss, looking first at the photograph, then at her. But he couldn't

FIGURE 6 Kate Duchêne's Jessica curls up in a comfortable armchair to avoid the advice of David Calder's Shylock. The photograph of her mother is visible on the side table. (2.5, 1993)

stop lecturing her, and when he said 'Fast bind', she jumped in with 'Fast find', as if trying to get him out of the house. There was a brief silence, and then he concluded, slightly embarrassed, 'A proverb never stale in thrifty mind' (2.5.51, 53, 54).

In addition to investing this short scene with a variety of extra-textual gestures to represent more fully the nuances of the Shylock/Jessica relationship, directors have inserted into productions a completely non-textual scene, though one which has a distinguished theatrical background. Patrick Stewart refers to 'Shylock's return', the moment when he comes home 'to find his house bereft of daughter, jewels and ducats' (Stewart, 13), as a possible sixth scene for Shylock. This moving scene was invented by Henry Irving, and was described by Ellen Terry, his Portia: 'the stage was empty, desolate, with no light but a pale moon, and all sounds of life at a great distance – and then over the bridge came the weary figure of the Jew' (quoted in Gross, 149). Gross continues the description: 'He was bearing a lantern, returning (though he did not realize it yet) to a deserted house. Then the curtain fell again, without a word having been spoken. In later performances, Irving extended the scene by having Shylock knock at the door, but either way the effect was piercing' (149). Much of the scene's effectiveness came from seeing the solitary figure on stage after it had been filled with an elaborate masquing scene, showing Jessica's elopement in the midst of musicians, dancers and pierrots. Herbert Beerbohm Tree, playing Shylock in 1908, extended the pathos of the scene – or so he thought – by breaking the silence with anguished cries of 'Jessica' as he ran through the empty house; Tree's Shylock then reappeared, 'flung himself on the ground, and tore his garments and sprinkled ashes on his head' (Lelyveld, 100).

Excessive as these additions may have seemed – and they disappeared from most of the Stratford productions of the play, with the exception of the 1947 production – they nonetheless focused on the pain caused to Shylock by Jessica's elopement. And as more recent productions have tried to show that Shylock's behaviour is motivated not simply by greed or hatred, they have reinvented Irving's interpolated scene. In 1993, David Calder's Shylock found himself literally surrounded by the crowd of party-goers blocking the stairs, keeping him from entering his house; the loud, raucous music seemed an added assault on the man who listened to Brahms in the safety of the home he was about to find empty. Like Beerbohm Tree, he called out for the missing Jessica. Gregory Doran's 1997 production made the masque not merely an occasion for dancing and music, but for pointedly anti-Semitic behaviour; the masquers wore pig masks, a reveller on platform shoes deliberately rubbed the mezuzah carved over Shylock's doorway with a string of sausages, and the riotous crowd swarmed around the returning Shylock. As he fought to get free, he suddenly confronted a figure carried on the shoulders of the rioters – Jessica, her hat snatched off, her long hair streaming down, her treachery clearly revealed to her father who could only cry out 'Jessica' before she was hurried away by Lorenzo and others. The happy festivities of Irving's Venice turned even uglier as Philip Voss's Shylock entered the house, only to find it spinning around. The audience watched Shylock being rocked from side to side, both physically and emotionally, until the house turned up stage, so that he disappeared from the audience's view. And, if one had a moment to notice details amid the swirling dancers and the spinning house, there was Bassanio, embracing a whore, enjoying himself on his last evening in Venice, before setting out for Belmont.

NOTE

1 What value, in contemporary terms, one assigns to the sum of three thousand ducats varies considerably. The programme for the 1998 production at Shakespeare's Globe asserted, without citing any sources, that 'Three thousand Ducats is approximately £350,000 in today's money'. That seems extremely high, but the problem is to figure out both what a ducat was worth in Shakespeare's time, and then what that value would be today. Thomas Coryate's book about his Italian travels, *Coryate's Crudities*, published in 1611, valued the ducat at about 4 shillings and 8 pence. W. Moelwyn Merchant, in his New Penguin edition, starts with this figure, estimates that three thousand ducats would have been worth £600–800, and then multiplies that figure by 25 to get to a sum of £20,000.

2

THE VENETIANS

I n trying to describe Shylock, one slides almost inevitably towards describing Jessica, since his relationship to his daughter is the most important aspect of his private life. But Shylock also has a public life, and one of the ways of understanding this complex figure is to move away from him, and towards the Venetians who hold social and political control, even if they lack financial stability and (sometimes) theatrical excitement. For when *The Merchant of Venice* begins, a first-time audience (which has not read the programme) may not even know that Shylock exists. Instead, the audience meets the citizens of Venice – Antonio, Salerio, Solanio (and occasionally Salarino), Gratiano, Lorenzo and Bassanio – all in the first scene. Later we will meet a Gaoler, the Duke and perhaps (depending on the production's budget and the director's choices) officers of the court, etc. And even before characters appear – or just as Antonio appears – twentieth-century audiences see a stage setting. That setting may be realistic, evoking actual images of one of the world's most picturesque cities, as in nineteenth-century productions; it may be a version of the 'real' Venice, perhaps using elements of the city, as Komisarjevsky did in his designs for the 1932 production, only now skewed and tilted to form an extravagantly comic version of bridges and towers. Venice may be romanticized as in Alan Tagg's 'brilliant scenery' for the 1956 production (Figure 7), where the play opened 'with a gay Venetian street scene, rich in colour and

FIGURE 7 Alan Tagg's first Venice setting in the 1956 production evokes an airy and romanticized Venice, with a gondola partially visible and cut-out structures representing the balconied houses that crown the Grand Canal. Figure 1 shows the set as it looked on stage.

beneath blue Italian skies' (*Warwick Adv.*), or created through less exotic details as in 1987 when wooden walkways similar to those leading to the canals formed the principal acting areas. Michael Langham's 1960 production moved the play into the eighteenth century, a time of elegant and showy clothing. Often the setting presents the mercantile world of the play, whether in the 1993 set suggesting a contemporary office world, complete on the upper level with working fax machines and computers (Figure 8), or in the 1997 production which first showed us a series of Venetian characters, from merchants holding bills of lading and talking with potential customers about the huge wrapped objects on stage to prostitutes soliciting customers. And at times the setting abstracts the notion of wealth and commerce, as in 1971, when gold and silver were the dominant colours in a setting Irving Wardle described as 'something between a royal Egyptian tomb and a bank vault', where 'Venice is introduced with a game of Rialto Monopoly played with golden ships on a mosaic floor' (*Times*, 1 Apr 1971).

FIGURE 8 The major feature of Shelagh Keegan's 1993 set was the metallic structure of poles and staircases. Several work stations are visible on the upper levels, complete with desks and computers. Downstage is the café table for the play's opening scene (see also Figure 9).

Whatever the designer's choices, the Venice of the named characters (as contrasted with any extras) seems an exclusively male society. No one is married, although Bassanio is thinking about it – and to a woman who lives somewhere else, in Belmont. No one mentions a mother, daughter, sister – except of course for Shylock, who remembers his wife Leah, and who loses his daughter Jessica, and Shylock's servant, Launcelot Gobbo, who calls himself 'an honest woman's son' and then even names his mother, Margery (2.2.15, 85). Within this male-dominated and male-focused world, we discern several overlapping groups, connected through their association with Antonio, the play's title role. In performance, Antonio himself is almost always separated from the others, by looks, age or costume. In 1956, Anthony Nicholls was dark and bearded in contrast to Basil Hoskins's blond Bassanio, who resembled 'a Greek god in disguise' (*S. Wales Arg.*).

Nicholls, who would return to the role at the National Theatre in 1970 was a 'sombre' figure (*Bristol E. Post*) unlike Hoskins's more open and likeable Bassanio (see Figure 1, p. 5). Frequently Antonio has been cast as older than Bassanio, perhaps as a hold-over from the source for the bond story, where the parallel figure, Ansaldo, is the godfather of the young man trying to wed the heiress, perhaps as a reflection of the standing he enjoys in Venice and the wealth he has amassed. But he can be older by ten years, as he was when David Bradley played him in 1978 to the Bassanio of John Nettles, or by fifteen as in the 1971 production, with Tony Church as Antonio and Michael Williams (later Bernard Lloyd) as Bassanio, or by thirty and more, as in the 1993 production with Clifford Rose's white-haired Antonio clearly in his late fifties or early sixties and Owen Teale's tousle-haired Bassanio in his late twenties (Figure 9). Depending on the age difference, he can seem an older brother (Bradley and Nettles, or, in 1981, Tom Wilkinson and Jonathan Hyde); he can be an avuncular figure (Church and Williams/Lloyd) (Figure 10); he can be a surrogate father (Rose and Teale, Julian Curry and Scott Handy in 1997).

One choice not taken in Stratford productions – or in any other production I've seen with the exception of David Bamber's middle-class Antonio in the 1999 National Theatre production – is to distinguish Antonio by class rather than by age or tempera-ment. Antonio normally appears in dark colours, the outward reflection of that mysterious sadness which is discussed for the first fifty-six lines of the play and which, since the play starts in mid-conversation, seems to have existed previously. Sometimes the dark colours are particularly evident, as in the 1984 production where the rest of the Venetians wore bright, even garish costumes decorated with sequins resembling (for several reviewers) matadors' outfits, while Christopher Ravenscroft's Antonio was in sequinned black, with a long black cape, or in 1971 when in the trial scene Tony Church's black-clad Antonio contrasted sharply with the white worn by Bassanio, fresh from

FIGURE 9 A white-haired Antonio (Clifford Rose) and his three obviously younger friends: the loquacious Gratiano (Mark Lockyer, standing centre), the resigned Lorenzo (Mark Lewis Jones) and a relaxed Bassanio (Owen Teale, right). (1.1, 1993)

his Belmont wooing. Sometimes the difference is less marked, as in 1981 when both Antonio (Tom Wilkinson) and Bassanio (Jonathan Hyde) wore dark colours, but Bassanio sported a flowing cape while Antonio wore a less flamboyant overcoat. But although Antonio looks more restrained, sombre, grave, mature – all of these adjectives float through reviews and discussions – he seems to be of the same social class as Bassanio, even though the latter is referred to as 'my Lord Bassanio', as if he's a nobleman, with all the money problems traditionally associated with that rank. In part, the lack of social distinction may be related to period costume, since modern audiences are unlikely to spot subtle differences. The 1993 modern-dress production at Stratford was able to distinguish Antonio and Bassanio, not only by age, but by financial status; Clifford Rose's Antonio seemed the type to have his own office while Owen

FIGURE 10 A sombre Antonio (Tony Church) listens to the appeal of Bassanio (Michael Williams) for money with which to woo Portia. Antonio's costumes were all in black, while Bassanio's coat was a patchwork of red and brown, accented by his light-coloured cape. (1.1, 1971)

Teale's Bassanio, more casually dressed, appeared to work in the general office, on the upper level of the unit set (see Figure 8, p. 46). And in 1999, at the Royal National Theatre, Trevor Nunn's production, set in the 1930s, presented a clear distinction between David Bamber's Antonio, who wore an ill-fitting blue suit and wire-rimmed glasses, and carried a briefcase, and everyone else, from Salerio and Solanio in their three-piece suits to a dapper young Bassanio; not only was this Antonio someone who worked (he actually looked like a clerk rather than a successful merchant), he was treated by the others as the man who would pay for their drinks.

Salerio and Solanio appear as an almost indivisible pair, showing up in the first scene with Antonio, then in the elopement scene with Lorenzo and Gratiano, then on their own to report on

Shylock's reaction to the elopement and then to confront Shylock directly. Their chiming/rhyming names, the uncertainty about whether there are three different characters or two characters and a printer's error, and their lack of direct involvement in or influence on the plot, have caused them to be known somewhat dismissively as 'the Salads' or 'the Sallies'.[1] They seem to be friends of Antonio's, but not as close to him as Bassanio, Gratiano and Lorenzo, if the line (from Salerio/Salarino) can be believed: 'I would have stay'd till I had made you merry, / If worthier friends had not prevented me' (1.1.60–1). Like Rosencrantz and Guildenstern, they can seem indistinguishable, even, in Gregory Doran's words, 'a sort of Italian Tweedledum and Tweedledee' (Doran, 70). In 1987, Doran himself played a Solanio noticeably younger than Michael Cadman's Salerio and a modish fashion plate as well.

Bassanio, Gratiano and Lorenzo clearly form a different group and one made up of three very different young men (see Figure 9, p. 48). Bassanio is described as Antonio's 'most noble kinsman' (1.1.57), although there are no further allusions to a blood relationship; Gratiano, characterized immediately as a loudmouth talker (he erupts into a 25-line speech beginning, 'Let me play the fool', 79–104), seems at first closer to Lorenzo, whom he takes off to dinner, and with whom he helps to organize Jessica's elopement, but he also insists that he must accompany Bassanio to Belmont. Lorenzo, overwhelmed by Gratiano's talking in scene 1, comes briefly into his own in Act 2 as Jessica's lover, and then retreats somewhat into the background. Most productions have played these three as relatively similar in age and appearance, although Bassanio, because he's the central figure for the plot, is often distinguished by looks (Scott Handy's fair hair setting him apart from a bearded Gratiano and a dark Lorenzo in 1997) or costume (Nicholas Farrell's beige-and-blue costume in 1987 noticeably lighter than those of the other men).

Of all the relationships, the most important is the one between Bassanio and Antonio, since the main plot depends on Antonio's willingness to enter into the bond with Shylock in order to get money for Bassanio, and even to die as a result of that bond. For many years, critics stressed the notion of male friendship as a Platonic ideal ('god-like amity' is Lorenzo's description at 3.4.3) revered by Elizabethans; they pointed to all the lines in the text which refer to Antonio's goodness; and they emphasized the self-sacrifice which Antonio seems willing to embrace for the sake of Bassanio (Brown, xlv–xlvi). But scholars have also noted less attractive qualities in Antonio, and the way in which they may shape the Antonio/Bassanio friendship: Antonio's mysterious sadness, the focus of discussions for the first fifty-five lines of the play; his tendency to remind Bassanio, first in his letter and then in his 'farewell' speech at the trial, of the huge debt (not so much of money as of gratitude) that Bassanio owes him; the touch of self-loathing in his description of himself as 'a tainted wether of the flock / Meetest for death' (4.1.114–15).[2] Is there any way to bring together these possibly contradictory views and assessments of Antonio, and his feelings for Bassanio?

Increasingly, directors and actors, as well as critics, have seen the Antonio/Bassanio relationship as one which first threatens and then is threatened by the Bassanio/Portia relationship. No actor today can overlook the evasiveness with which Bassanio responds to Antonio's question, 'what lady is the same / To whom you swore a secret pilgrimage – / That you to-day promis'd to tell me of' (1.1.119–21). For almost forty lines, Bassanio dodges around the tricky subject of asking for money before he says, 'In Belmont is a lady richly left', and then, 'Her name is Portia' (161, 165). Bassanio's unwillingness to answer the question directly – and Antonio has to keep asking Bassanio to tell him what he wants – is evident on the page. On the stage, the actor playing Bassanio normally moves away from Antonio, doesn't look at him directly and searches for words that will convince. He never actually mentions money, but instead constructs a long speech about shooting one arrow after others that have gone astray, a moment that felt completely appropriate for Scott Handy's young, naive Bassanio of 1997 (Figure 11). Given Antonio's unexplained

FIGURE 11 Bassanio (Scott Handy) gestures to illustrate his metaphor of shooting one arrow to find another one (1.1.140–52), while a gaunt and clearly older Antonio (Julian Curry) listens to his young friend. (1997)

sadness, his short – and often brusque – dismissal of the notion that this sadness is because he is 'in love', and the fact that 'to-day' is the day Bassanio has promised to tell him of his 'secret pilgrimage', one wonders whether Antonio and Bassanio both realize that the possibility of marriage will change, perhaps even destroy, their friendship.

Such a reading leads to the interpretation which first appeared at Stratford in 1965, and has featured increasingly since then, namely that the Antonio/Bassanio relationship is a homoerotic one, usually one-sided (Antonio loves Bassanio) and often unacknowledged. The basis for this choice lies in the text, but also in the way one interprets the text, especially the word 'love', which recurs frequently in conversations between Antonio and Bassanio. In the first scene of the play, Bassanio refers to his debts to Antonio, both 'in money and in love':

> to you, Antonio,
> I owe the most in money and in love,
> And from your love I have a warranty
> To unburthen all my plots and purposes
> How to get clear of all the debts I owe.
>
> (130–4)

Antonio also speaks of love when he questions Bassanio about the name of the lady, claiming that Bassanio ought to trust him: 'You know me well, and herein spend but time / To wind about my love with circumstance' (153–4). When Antonio writes to Bassanio, telling him that the bond is forfeit, he again appeals to love, this time implying that Bassanio should feel guilty for his absence:

> Sweet Bassanio, my ships have all miscarried, my creditors grow cruel, my estate is very low, my bond to the Jew is forfeit; and since in paying it, it is impossible I should live, all debts are clear'd between you and I, if I might but see you at my death: notwithstanding, use your pleasure, – if your love do not persuade you to come, let not my letter.   (3.2.314–20)

Crucially, after the lawyer (Portia in disguise) who has saved Antonio's life leaves, having asked for the ring Bassanio wears, and having been refused, Antonio again presses the claims of love:

> My Lord Bassanio, let him have the ring,
> Let his deservings and my love withal
> Be valued 'gainst your wife's commandement.
>
> (4.1.445–7)

Antonio specifically asks Bassanio to choose between his promise to his wife and his debt to Antonio, thus underlining the struggle for possession of Bassanio's love. And in the play's final scene, though Bassanio defends his giving away of Portia's ring as something he had to do, he still never directly mentions Antonio's request:

> I was enforc'd to send it after him,
> I was beset with shame and courtesy,
> My honour would not let ingratitude
> So much besmear it:
>
> (5.1.216–19)

Passive verbs and abstract nouns, but never the clear statement, 'Antonio asked me to give away the ring.' Is he unwilling to embarrass his friend? Or unwilling to admit to Portia that someone else is more important than she is?

The foregrounding of a homosexual relationship has developed gradually, first in criticism, then in performance.[3] At the RSC, the idea of a homosexual relationship emerged in the 1965 production, where Brewster Mason's Antonio (Mason took over from a sick William Squire) was, in B.A. Young's description, 'the counterpart of today's wealthy bachelor stockbroker', an Antonio who, 'even in imminent danger from Shylock's knife, ... keeps his eyes affectionately fixed on the boy-friend whose extravagance has brought him to this situation' (*FT*). To Penelope Gilliatt (*Observer*) 'Antonio's homosexual love for Bassanio' was 'as plain and simple in the play as the blocks of Ralph Koltai's beautiful sets', while R.B. Marriott noted that 'the homosexual thread of the relationship between Antonio and Bassanio is revealed naturally and easily' (*Stage & TV*). Other reviewers of the 1965 production seemingly saw no such relationship, speaking only of the 'solid' (*Oxf. Mail*) or 'subdued and austere' Antonio (*S. Wales E. Arg.*). Tony Church's Antonio in the 1971 production had a similar subtext, although so muted that Gareth Lloyd Evans complained, 'the producer should by now have decided whether the character is homosexual or not – Mr Church does not seem at all sure' (*Guardian*). Other reviewers read the performance more clearly, while still noting its subtlety. David Isaacs praised Church's 'exceptional' performance, saying, 'He manages throughout to exude the deep-rooted sadness of Antonio and even hints at its sexual overtones without spelling out too stark a message' (*Coventry E. Tel.*), while Irving Wardle noted a similar balance in Antonio: 'As Tony Church plays him there is no question of his love for Bassanio, but it is a melancholy understanding of love with no physical expression; thus it becomes acceptable within the production's romantic terms' (*Times*, 1 Apr). And R.B. Marriott shows how the actor linked the two major issues of the role: 'Tony Church is a somewhat melancholy Antonio, not only upset because of his awful predicament but on account of his lonely love for Bassanio' (*Stage*). When asked by Norrie Epstein, 'Is he gay?' Church replied: 'You're not to know this entirely' but pointed out that Shakespeare had changed the sources, where Antonio is 'either a godfather or stepfather. Shakespeare deliberately ignores these possibilities, thereby opening up the possibility of Antonio as Bassanio's lover' (Epstein, 108).

When I saw this production in London in 1973, long before this book was ever conceived, I remember thinking that the Antonio/Bassanio relationship was more than just a friendship, in large part because of the age difference between the two men. Tony Church seemed obviously a man in his early forties, while Bernard Lloyd (who took over the role of Bassanio from Michael Williams) was clearly in his late twenties or early thirties; the age gap, together with the kiss Bassanio bestowed casually on Antonio when he entered (as contrasted with the handshake for Solanio), somehow implied a special connection, more than friends, different from relations. Perhaps the subtext was evident also because of Jonathan Miller's production at the National Theatre in 1970 where an older Antonio, proper in a late Victorian frock coat (Antony Nicholls seemed in his fifties while Jeremy Brett's Bassanio was in his late thirties), would evoke 'the relationship between Oscar Wilde and Bosie where a sad old queen regrets the opportunistic heterosexual love of a person whom he adored' (Miller, 107).

At any rate, from the early 1970s on, hinting at Antonio's repressed homosexual love for Bassanio became a fairly standard reading, both on the stage and in critical articles. In 1987, Bill Alexander's RSC production took that reading much further; there was no guessing about whether or not John Carlisle's Antonio loved Nicholas Farrell's Bassanio, whether one heard the curt tone of 'Fie, fie' (1.1.46) as he dismissed the speculation that he might be in love in a voice that indicated 'keep off this subject', or watched his sad face as Bassanio talked about Portia, or noted that once

Antonio agreed to search for the necessary funds, Bassanio hugged Antonio who responded by kissing him on the lips. But this production also strongly implied that Bassanio knew of Antonio's love and was willing to exploit it in order to get the money he needed. Again, the playing of the first Antonio/Bassanio scene was crucial. Bassanio initiated all the approaches to Antonio, moving towards him as he spoke of his debts, taking his arms on 'to you Antonio / I owe the most in money and in love' (130–1), the physical gesture inevitably emphasizing the debt in love. Antonio kept moving away, Bassanio kept following him, almost as if he knew that his physical proximity would help to convince Antonio to listen to him. When Bassanio finally spoke of Portia, he nonetheless kept physical contact with Antonio, standing behind him and putting his hands on Antonio's shoulders, then kneeling beside him. And while this first scene ended with Bassanio's hugging Antonio in exuberant pleasure, and being kissed by Antonio, it was Bassanio, at the end of 1.3, when Shylock and Antonio have agreed to the bond, who kissed Antonio, as if recognizing that he owed him not only money but also his love.

Alexander further emphasized the homosexual relationship between Antonio and Bassanio by mirroring it with the Salerio/Solanio relationship, where again the audience saw a middle-aged man (Michael Cadman's Salerio) in love with a younger man (Gregory Doran's Solanio). Doran, a player of relatively small roles during the 1987 RSC season, who has since become a director for the RSC, has written perceptively, and humorously, about playing Solanio, noting that it's Solanio who says, when trying to fathom the cause of Antonio's sadness, 'Why then you are in love' (1.1.46). And again, it's Solanio, points out Doran, who says of Antonio's sorrow at Bassanio's leaving, 'I think he only loves the world for him' (2.8.50). In the 1987 production, both men were richly dressed, and Solanio was especially noticeable with 'an ostentatious pearl rosary, commas of rouge on the cheeks, kohl on the eyes, and a pickadevant [i.e. trimmed to a point] beard and moustache' (Doran, 71).

Even more striking was the playing of the short scene (2.8) in which Salerio and Solanio describe offstage events – Shylock's reaction to the flight of Jessica, with money and jewels, and the departure of Bassanio from Venice. The first part of the scene contained the usual imitation of Shylock, with the mockery made especially easy by the pronounced accent Antony Sher used as Shylock. In the second half of the scene, however, as Salerio described the parting of Bassanio from Antonio, he used the physical details as an excuse to try to touch – and seduce – Solanio. Solanio reclined centre stage – was this gesture an invitation to something? – and Salerio first knelt beside him, then touched his elbow, then (on 'He wrung Bassanio's hand', 49) fondled his right hand, but Solanio moved away from him. The offstage action described and the action taking place on stage merged in a disturbing way, not necessarily because of the mirroring effect (although doubtless some members of the audience found the whole idea of homosexual couples offensive), but because we saw how Salerio was exploiting – perhaps even inventing – the description for his own purposes. And the rejection, not in words, but in action, by Solanio, was also disturbing, since it seemed that the younger man had, by lying down, led Salerio to expect a response that he then did not get.

In his admirable study of *The Merchant of Venice* in performance, James C. Bulman argues that Alexander's production encouraged the audience's prejudices, especially in relation to homosexuality: 'he makes us queasy about siding with the Venetians against Shylock not only because they are so calculatedly dishonest with one another, but because their dishonesty is bound up in stereotypes of homosexual behaviour that culturally "enlightened" audiences have been taught to disavow' (Bulman, 128). He's certainly right, but the Salerio/Solanio interpretation, while mirroring the Antonio/Bassanio relationship, also stood in contrast to it, because Farrell's Bassanio finally came to realize just how exploitative his behaviour had been (see p.103).

The Alexander production, and Carlisle's Antonio, mark the extreme which more recent Antonios have stepped back from. Clifford Rose in 1993 was a dapper, white-haired, Stock Exchange Antonio, covering his feelings. Julian Curry in 1997, lean, almost gaunt, avoided physical contact with Bassanio (though he didn't shrink from the embraces of Lorenzo and Gratiano when they left), as if knowing he couldn't hide his feelings if that close to him, and only touched him in the trial scene when, convinced that he was about to die, he gave his farewell speech clinging to Bassanio, and stroking his back.

Most Bassanios charm the audience through good looks and youth. Even Scott Handy's entrance in 1997, preceded by shouts and laughter, and culminating in a stumbling fall on to the stage, caused apparently by drinking (he carried a small hip flask), though clearly not the entrance of 'your most noble kinsman', was an index of his youth and naiveté and, in this case, anxiety. But Bassanio also seems more acceptable to an audience which judges him not only by his behaviour with Antonio but in contrast to Gratiano. For in Gratiano, Shakespeare has created a foil to Bassanio, similar in that he goes to Belmont and finds a wife, but quite different in his talkativeness, in his vulgarity and, often, in his viciousness. It's a 'sidekick' role which may help explain, quietly, why Bassanio finds it pleasant to be in Antonio's company; Gratiano, as Bassanio says, 'speaks an infinite deal of nothing (more than any man in all Venice)' (1.1.114–15). Shakespeare gives him what amounts to a star entrance, since he comes in and immediately launches into a 25-line speech which offers an actor the opportunity to show off his wit and imagination. Beginning with 'Let me play the fool' (79), Gratiano attempts to cheer up Antonio by making him laugh at his own melancholy. The speech is reminiscent of (though less highly image-crammed than) Mercutio's Queen Mab speech, in which Mercutio tries to divert and tease Romeo out of his 'I don't want to go to the party' mood – and indeed the Gratiano of the 1993 production, Mark Lockyer, returned to Stratford in 1995 to play

Mercutio. Gratiano's appearance normally creates a sense of bustle and noise, whether he is taking a cigarette away from Antonio (John Bowe in 1978) or sketching a likeness of Antonio as he talks (Geoffrey Freshwater in 1987) or getting quickly drunk at Antonio's expense and having to be taken off by Lorenzo (Lockyer in 1993). And while the text of the play certainly gives Gratiano the opportunity to be voluble, the trend in production has been to make him noisy, often irritating, occasionally violent.

That trend is not one imposed or imagined by directors, since the idea of Gratiano-as-noise-maker comes directly from the text. When Gratiano insists that he must accompany Bassanio to Belmont, Bassanio at first refuses – 'Thou art too wild, too rude, and bold of voice' (2.2.172) – and warns Gratiano that his 'skipping spirit' and 'wild behaviour' (178) may embarrass Bassanio. Gratiano doesn't argue with the description, but promises instead to 'put on a sober habit' (181), thus promising to 'act' the part, both in behaviour and in dress. But, as he says, 'I bar to-night, you shall not gauge me / By what we do to-night' (190–1). And the staging of the 'abduction' of Jessica (2.6) has frequently been a chance to add music and dancing to the text. Pre-opening publicity for Michael Benthall's 1947 production described the show as a 'balletic fantasy', but the *Manchester Guardian* seemed relieved to find only a 'modest carnival scene'. Nonetheless, the masquers, with both large and small red and white streamers, plus sticks with red and black feathers, came down the steps swirling around Jessica, Lorenzo, Gratiano and Salerio, throwing the streamers into the centre of the stage, and giving point to Lorenzo's lines, 'on gentlemen, away! / Our masquing mates by this time for us stay' (2.6.58–9) (Figure 12). More ominously, after the short dialogue between Antonio and Gratiano that concludes the scene, the masquers returned to dance again. Shylock entered and tried to go up the steps to his house, but found the dancers blocking his way. Fighting his way through them, he entered the house while the dancers continued to circle around; his re-entrance was a run down the steps, clearly

FIGURE 12 The elopement of Jessica and Lorenzo in 1947 took place as masquers filled the stage. Foreground, a masked Lorenzo (Donald Sinden) stretches out his hand to Jessica (Joy Parker), wearing men's clothes. Upstage of them, Gratiano (Myles Eason, striped doublet) watches, and behind Jessica is Salarino (John Warner). (2.6)

looking for his missing daughter, while the dancers circled once more and the interval curtain fell.

Later productions, with smaller casts and thus fewer people to use as extra dancers, have often turned the carnival aspect of the scene into something much less graceful and much more obnoxious. In 1978, John Bowe's Gratiano kicked his heels in anticipation of pleasure when he said 'I bar to-night', and then gave a loud howl as he exited. When he returned, to assist Lorenzo with the abduction/elopement of Jessica, he entered riding on Solanio's back. Not only did Gratiano, Lorenzo, Salerio and Solanio have masks for the scene, but also capguns, which they shot off playfully. B.A. Young described the group as 'a bunch of young Venetian layabouts whose vulgar and noisy high spirits is [sic] beyond bearing. Gratiano (John Bowe) is their intolerable leader, a man whose loudmouthed crudity would stand out in a West Ham football crowd; but they are all willing to go along with him in their rowdy fun' (FT, Warehouse transfer). When Barton restaged this production in 1981, on the main stage at Stratford, the masquers now carried – and played – musical instruments, so that instead of quick shots, the audience heard a cacophony of noise from Solanio's bugle, Salerio's cymbals, Gratiano's trombone and Launcelot Gobbo's drum. In addition to the noise, the masks and cloaks worn by the masquers heightened the sense of 'a jeering, mocking herd' as Rosalind Carne called them (FT); the 'garish colours are all the more tasteless for the overall muted creams, browns and golds of the design – visual substance to his [Shylock's] earlier warnings that she [Jessica] should shut up the casements'.

In 1987, Gratiano's entrance to meet Bassanio was marked by an upstage moment when he slapped one of the street people as he entered, an act of gratuitous violence. His exuberance at hearing that he could go to Belmont showed itself with a huge hug for Bassanio; Gratiano actually picked him up and had to be pushed away. Bassanio's description of Gratiano's 'skipping spirit' seemed very apt, and yet the companionable touching between the two suggested that Bassanio enjoyed Gratiano's company. In the elopement scene, Gratiano's merry-making moved towards vulgarity. The promptbook direction is eloquent: 'As they exit, Jessica and Lorenzo stop on bridge for quick kiss. Gr[atiano] re-enters, barking, bites J's bum. L and J exit, leaving Gr on bridge, looking at casket.'

And in 1993, Gratiano (Mark Lockyer) was not just a talkative exhibitionist, but someone who verged on being seriously out of control. His request to Bassanio to go to Belmont was made in the 'office' setting – and when he was told he could go, he vigorously waved a champagne bottle, frequently spraying the computers on the desks and sometimes the other actors. The stage manager's nightly reports on the show indicate that the champagne occasionally even stopped the fax machine from working, and the scene was reblocked when the production moved to Newcastle in an attempt to safeguard the equipment. Gratiano's punning reference to Jessica, 'Now (by my hood) a gentle, and no Jew' (2.6.51), casually thrown out as Jessica prepared to join them, received an angry comeback, almost a putdown, from Lorenzo: 'Beshrew me but I love her heartily' – with the adverb stressed so that Gratiano – and we – could hear that Lorenzo wasn't prepared to take that kind of slur even from a friend. Later, in the trial scene, when Gratiano verbally attacks Shylock, this Gratiano went further and attacked him physically; his friends had to pull him away. It became clear that behaviour which, in the first half of the play, might be attributed to an extrovert personality and some heavy drinking, now seemed potentially self-destructive, as if the messy hair, the unkempt appearance and the violent threats were signals of a breakdown, whether caused by drink, or drugs, or just the stress of the situation.

Textually, the most pointed and vicious anti-Semitic remarks in the play come from Gratiano. But productions have also demonstrated that the hatred of the Jew-as-outsider is an aspect of the entire society, not simply confined to a single character. Henry Irving made the violence part of the trial scene, adding some nameless Jews who were jeered at by the crowd and forced into a corner by guards. And after Irving's dignified exit, the Jews left as well, followed by a group of Christians, and yells were heard, as if the persecution was now continuing offstage. The twentieth-century tendency has been to make that offstage persecution visible on stage. In 1965, not surprisingly, it was Gratiano who drew a dagger on Shylock as he cursed him: 'for thy desires / Are wolvish, bloody, starv'd, and ravenous' (4.1.137–8). And when Shylock tried to leave the court after realizing that he would get nothing at all – 'I'll stay no longer question' (342) – guards stopped him, and the crowd closed in. Solanio and an unnamed lawyer brought him back to centre stage, while the guards restrained the still angry crowd. By 1971, Bassanio seems to have joined in the visible persecution, spitting at Shylock after Shylock rejected the bag holding six thousand ducats; the gesture punctuated Shylock's question, 'What judgment shall I dread, doing no wrong?' (89) and Shylock's response, to drop the bag of money in front of Bassanio, emphasized his words about the Venetians thinking they could use slaves like animals because they 'bought them' (92).

In 1987, the persecution moved beyond the trial scene, and came from a much wider range of characters. Before a word of the play had been spoken, two Venetian gallants entering up stage spat at a lone Jew (Tubal) identifiable as such from the yellow Mogen David on his shoulder as they crossed by him; that casually contemptuous gesture was the central one of the play, repeated frequently. After Shylock agreed to lend Antonio money and hurried off to get it, Antonio spat after him. Venetian ruffians, described in the promptbook as 'freaks', and led by Launcelot Gobbo, made a noise outside Shylock's house, for 2.5, playing a fanfare on whistles, echoing Launcelot's call of 'Why Jessica', laughing at Gobbo's jokes, following Shylock off stage as he finally left Jessica. These creatures – never clearly perceived or identified – became even more vicious; when Shylock entered in 3.1 to meet Salerio and Solanio, the 'freaks' were throwing stones at him, and a streak of blood on Antony Sher's forehead showed that one, at least, had struck. Looking at his pursuers, Sher's Shylock crashed into Solanio, then rebounded off to Salerio, then back to Solanio who pushed him to the ground. Gregory Doran (Solanio) describes the attack as 'vultures on a rattlesnake', and offers a chillingly repellent picture of their behaviour:

> We taunted and sneered at the Jew, shoving him between us, and knocked him to the ground: 'You knew, none so well, none so well

as you, of my daughter's flight' [3.1.22–3]. Even Shylock knows of his assailants' reputations. The Salads are proud of their part in the scam, and brag about it, gloating over Shylock's misery. We prodded him with a stick, as if he were a poisonous scorpion, until he scuttled out of reach.   (Doran, 73–4)

Shylock was bleeding even before this attack (Figure 13) but that did not stop the Salads; a moment later they held the stick under his chin as a kind of torture instrument. And, of course, after Shylock responded with enormous anger and threats of vengeance, they took out their abashed frustration on Tubal once again, spitting on him as he entered, and shouting 'Jew, Jew' as they left.

The trial scene in 1987 combined all of these elements: the 'freaks' jeering at Shylock as he entered, applauding all of Gratiano's angry words, chanting 'Jew, Jew'; the Venetians (Gratiano, Bassanio, Solanio, Salerio and the Gaoler) barring Shylock's entrance to the court, so much so that the Duke's 'Make room, and let him stand before our face' (4.1.16) was a needed command; the spitting (my notes show that Bassanio spat at Shylock on 'are you answered?', 62, while the promptbook records a sword-drawing gesture for Bassanio); the ganging up on Shylock, this time by Gratiano and Bassanio after he's defeated ('Bass and Gr grab Sh in armlock', reads the promptbook); and, as a final insult, Bassanio taking Shylock's hand and using it to make the sign of the cross.

We should note that the increased violence shown towards Shylock in this production was met by outrageous behaviour from him (see pp. 135–6). The more raucous and noisy the surrounding atmosphere became, the more overt hatred radiated from Shylock himself, as if viciousness fed and nourished more viciousness. And, not surprisingly, all of the productions with overt physical violence were set in 'period' costume. Gregory Doran offers an explanation:

After all, Shylock says he is frequently spat upon, spurned and kicked as a matter of course. When the play is transposed to a more genteel period, to a more polite society such as the Victorian or Edwardian era, it is difficult to convey the routine violence of this racism. (Doran, 72)

FIGURE 13 A bleeding Shylock (Antony Sher) is surrounded by Salerio (Michael Cadman) and Solanio (Gregory Doran, with stick) as they taunt him about Jessica's elopement. (3.1, 1987)

The productions that followed in 1993 and 1997 offer a clear example of the difference. In 1993, the physical violence came primarily from a disturbed Gratiano and the society's violence was aesthetic (loud rock music blared out during the abduction of Jessica). But in 1997, with a production set in Renaissance Venice, the abduction of Jessica became an occasion for gratuitously anti-Semitic behaviour (see p. 42).

Almost inevitably, the attacks on Shylock by the Venetians have a boomerang effect. Audiences read the Venetians as prejudiced – whether deliberately or casually so – and callous. Thus, in the second half of the twentieth century, the Venetians on stage have become more obviously the oppressors. In 1960, Robert Muller read the Venetians in their eighteenth-century setting as 'abominable Mozartian clubmen' (*D. Mail*) and *Punch*'s reviewer contrasted the 'appalling arrogance of Antonio and his caddish hangers-on' to O'Toole's Shylock, 'almost the only gentleman in Venice'. Whether dressed as versions of the watching audience, or as Georgian noblemen, Victorian gentlemen or Renaissance figures, the Venetians are no longer clearly the heroes, but, at times, may even seem to be the 'villains'.

NOTES

1 As both M.M. Mahood and Jay Halio make clear in their editions (New Cambridge and Oxford, respectively), one can make a reasonable case, both textually and dramatically, for the existence of three Venetians with similar-sounding names: Solanio (or sometimes Salanio) and Salarino, who appear together up to 3.1, and Salerio, who appears, textually, in 3.2. Most productions choose only two, usually Salerio and Solanio.
2 Robert Hapgood offers a useful, and representative, comment: 'Antonio is at once too generous and too possessive' (Hapgood, 26).
3 The homoerotic reading appears in Auden's essay, 'Brothers and others', and has been developed elsewhere. Lawrence Hyman, in the usefully titled essay, 'The rival lovers in *The Merchant of Venice*', suggests that whether or not Antonio has 'some unconscious sexual feeling for Bassanio', the important point is 'that Antonio feels rejected when he sees that his friend is determined to marry' (Hyman, 110).

3

THE PROBLEM OF LAUNCELOT GOBBO

There are lots of problems with Launcelot Gobbo, from the variant spellings of his name to the question of whether he is a hunchback (as *'gobbo'*, the Italian for hunchback, implies), to the larger question of what he's doing in the play. Indeed, Christopher Luscombe, one of the most successful Gobbos in recent memory at the RSC, indicated his distress at realizing, after accepting the role, that the part wasn't even mentioned in Lamb's *Tales from Shakespeare* (Luscombe, 1993). It's difficult to think of any other servant or messenger in a Shakespeare play who comes into the play without his 'master', and who is given a biography of his own, a small moral crisis and even a parent – and all before he actually does anything in relation to major characters. Though Launcelot seems at first merely a comic character, hopelessly given to puns and malapropisms, his seemingly callous treatment, first of his blind father and then later of Jessica, raise questions for the audience.

Even his physical appearance requires a choice, for, side-stepping the question of whether or not he's a hunchback, the text offers two noticeably conflicting views of his size. Launcelot describes himself as 'famish'd' in Shylock's service, and if we unscramble his line, 'You may tell every finger I have with my ribs' (2.2.102–3), we find the implication that he's so thin his ribs are visibly present. But Shylock warns him that he will not be able to eat so much when he serves Bassanio ('thou shalt not gormandize

/ As thou hast done with me', 2.5.3–4) and describes Launcelot as a 'huge feeder' (2.5.45). Clearly each version is self-serving, Launcelot justifying his leaving by his 'starvation', Shylock justifying Launcelot's departure by the savings he will thus accrue. Most Launcelots have been on the thin side, whether the ragged street-urchin look of Phil Daniels in 1987 (one of whose other roles that season was the slave Ithamore in *The Jew of Malta*, purchased because he's 'leaner' and therefore cheaper), or the slender Christopher Luscombe (looking young enough to play, in the same season, the page Moth in *Love's Labour's Lost)*. Jimmy Chisholm, the 1997 Launcelot, had a small pot-belly, and John Garley, in 1956, had a round face and plumpish body – perhaps only 'semi-huge' eaters. The most grotesque – physically – was the 1984 Launcelot of Brian Parr, hunchbacked (as was his father, Old Gobbo), and given to doing 'funny voices' now and then.

The typical solution to playing Launcelot Gobbo has been to fall back on the textual identification of the stage direction which brings him on stage: *'Enter ... the clown alone'* (2.2.0). Editors usually gloss *clown* as 'rustic', someone from the country rather than from the city (John Garley in 1956 was clearly a 'country bumpkin' according to Rosemary Anne Sisson, *SA Herald*) but the temptation to read *clown* as equivalent to 'fool' is almost irresistible. And, like other fools in Shakespeare, Launcelot talks to the audience (cf. Launce in *The Two Gentlemen of Verona*), puns incessantly (Speed in *The Two Gentlemen of Verona*, as well as Launce, and the two Dromios in *The Comedy of Errors*) and misuses language (Bottom in *A Midsummer Night's Dream*, Dogberry in *Much Ado About Nothing*). His opening monologue as he debates the rights and wrongs of leaving Shylock is, on one level, a bravura piece for a stand-up comedian, especially one who can do different voices for the conscience and the devil. Indeed, the National Theatre's 1999 production of *The Merchant of Venice* removed Launcelot's monologue from its usual place and moved it several scenes later where it was performed in a cabaret as a comic turn. The dialogue with oneself is an old *commedia dell'arte* routine

(Arlecchino contemplating suicide, for example) and that background, plus the Venetian setting for the play, supports a reading of Launcelot as a figure who is performed as a traditional comic character: Donald Pleasence in 1953, sporting a 'ginger untidy wig', according to the costume chart, was clearly in that tradition. John Garley (1956) impressed John Wardle (*Bolton E. News*) who, in a long and thoughtful review, commented on Launcelot's undeserved reputation as one of the 'feebler Shakesperian [*sic*] clowns' and argued that the part is 'an opportunity... to the really accomplished comedian' such as Mr Garley. Charles Kay in 1965 appeared at first with his 'behind literally sticking out of his tights' (*Oxf. Mail*) but still seemed 'a nimble, ever-smiling Launcelot Gobbo' (*Coventry E. Tel.*). Peter Geddis, in 1971, was 'a sad whey-faced clown' (*Yorks. Post*) and 'a *commedia dell'arte* clown' (*FT*).

If these Launcelots were primarily physical comedians, the Launcelot Gobbo of the two John Barton productions, 1978 and 1981, was essentially an entertainer – a one-man band (as Ned Chaillet called him in 1978, *Times*), playing first a squeeze box, then a penny whistle, then a lute and even a horn, as he punctuated his opening monologue with sound effects (Figure 14). For B.A. Young, Hilton McRae's Launcelot Gobbo was a major success, 'an effervescent comic' and a 'wholly likeable character' (*FT*). Other reviewers cited Harpo Marx as an inspiration, though Peter Jenkins found him 'most unfunnily acted' (*Spectator*), while Marina Warner (*Vogue*) seemed much more positive about the 'humming, strumming, improvising madcap Hilton McRae'. The instruments made the scene with Old Gobbo into a kind of musical comic turn, with Launcelot showing off his assorted collection either as distractions or as brief emphatic comments. Thus, the line 'I am sure Margery your wife is my mother' (2.2.85–6) is underscored by Launcelot playing what the promptbook refers to as 'the conscience theme'. By the scene's end, when father and son are finally united, the promptbook direction is 'Both play tune and sing' – with Old Gobbo turning out to be a squeezebox-player

FIGURE 14 Launcelot Gobbo (Hilton McRae) was a one-man band in 1978; here he plays the guitar and has the squeeze-box to hand while he sings nonsense to his blind father. (2.2, 1978)

as well. The music, as Marina Warner noted, 'adds to the atmosphere of lightheartedness' especially when Launcelot's teasing of Jessica in 3.5 became another musical number, as he sang 'for in converting Jews to Christians, you raise the price of pork' (31–3). Avril Carson's Jessica, though not protesting the joke, nonetheless felt hurt by his musical teasing (Carson in conversation with me). And even Lorenzo's attempt to implicate Launcelot in some offstage hanky-panky with a Moorish servant simply provided Launcelot with another singing opportunity, strumming chords as he improvised a tune to 'It is much that the Moor should be more than reason' (37–8).

When Barton directed the play three years later (1981) for the main house in Stratford, he kept the notion of Launcelot as an entertainer, although Rob Edwards had only a guitar while Old Gobbo now held the concertina, with a begging tin attached to it.

At one point during rehearsals, some sort of elaborate gag must have been planned, since the props list of 25 February 1981 contains the following items:

> Birdcage with shoulder strap with dead parrot in. Cage to be openable from top. 2 bottles of beer, beer bottle opener. Launcelot takes these from his coat pocket and opens them onstage. Bottles and cage get thrown on floor, Launcelot then puts bottles in cage.

A month later, the production notes for 28 March 1981 record the demise of the dead parrot and beer joke: 'Birdcage for parrot, 2 beer bottles and bottle opener for Launcelot are cut.' A further note to the properties designer is helpful: 'Launcelot's bundle of belongings should be a haversack; it should be designed so that when Launcelot is walking and playing his guitar, the haversack can be slung over one shoulder and will not fall off.' Given the difficulties of managing haversack and guitar, one suspects that the birdcage, beer bottles and dead parrot may have been too much to manage – or too reminiscent of Monty Python?

But certainly the scene with Launcelot and his father was played for laughs, with Launcelot pulling his father around the stage as he gave him confusing directions. Thus the potentially troubling quality of the scene, even with an Old Gobbo wearing a 'blind' sign around his neck, became instead the opportunity for a comic turn. In the 1978 production, in The Other Place, Hilton McRae had moved around on his own, so perhaps the larger space of the main house generated larger movements. Certainly the stage itself offered the chance for Old Gobbo to walk off it – almost – into the audience, and seems to have produced Rob Edwards's memorable ad lib, 'Mind the canals' – but only at the first preview.

Making the scene between Launcelot and Old Gobbo essentially comic is one solution; cutting it, either partially or altogether, is another. The usual solution has been to trim the scene slightly, but, in 1997, the director completely eliminated Old Gobbo. Thus, after Jimmy Chisholm's Launcelot debated with himself about leaving Shylock and decided in favour of doing so, he used the phrase 'I will run' as an excuse for running around Shylock's house (a free-standing structure upstage centre). He then asserted, 'I'll to one Master Bassanio, who indeed gives rare new liveries', a line reworked from Launcelot's instruction to his father, 'give me your present to one Master Bassanio, who indeed gives rare new liveries' (2.2.103–5). The text's scene in which both father and son try to persuade Bassanio to take Launcelot as a servant, with Launcelot constantly interrupting his father, consequently shrank by half, and so the question of what Old Gobbo is doing in the play or what to do with this scene ceased to exist.

But, as Christopher Luscombe points out, the scene with Old Gobbo 'is not only a front-cloth sketch; it is also a comic version of the filial tensions in both Jessica and Portia's stories' (Luscombe, 1998). He notes the 'pain that Gobbo inflicts on his blind father' (23) without directly explaining why Launcelot Gobbo would behave in such a way. He's aware of the character's 'unattractive trait', but goes no further. Yet Luscombe's much praised portrayal of Launcelot, in 1993, as 'an outsider . . . in this ruthless, macho world', or a suburban boy 'in a world of urban sophistication' (Luscombe, 1998, 24) may offer a clue to his treatment of his father. Terrified of Shylock, sweating in his 'off the peg' blazer and pullover, he relishes the chance to be superior to someone – and that someone is his father. Besides, having just totally embarrassed himself by casually running his fingers over the computer keyboard at Shylock's elegant desk and completely scrambling everything there, his treatment of his father seemed a way to recover his sense of control (Figure 15).

Basing his interpretation on a sense of the character as being out of place, Luscombe then found that puns were often helpful and even created a new one. When Launcelot, in 2.3, said goodbye to Jessica with 'adieu', he added 'A Jew' and laughed at his own joke. As Luscombe pointed out, the pun shows 'both a lapse of taste and an instinctive verbal dexterity. He knew he shouldn't have said it, but he just couldn't resist it' (Luscombe,

FIGURE 15 Christopher Luscombe's Launcelot Gobbo sits at Shylock's desk, trying to look as if he knows what he is doing. (1993)

1998, 24). And neither could the next Launcelot on the main stage, Jimmy Chisholm, who picked up the same pun.

While Luscombe's essay on Launcelot indicates his awareness of the character's potential for causing pain, his playing of the role stressed the character's own insecurities. But Phil Daniels's young Cockney ruffian (1987) had no such inner qualms, and seemed to delight in his own aggressiveness (Figure 16). He boldly imitated Shylock's accent, 'Your worship was wont to tell me, I could do nothing without bidding' (2.5.8–9), right to Shylock's face, and joined with the ragged 'freaks' who served as a Jew-baiting chorus throughout. Not surprisingly, this Launcelot had an elongated cross tattooed on his arm. And although he played as a joke his lines to Jessica about the impossibility of her salvation (in 3.5) he certainly never noticed how upset those jokes made her. Even his exit to go off and prepare the serving of dinner had a strangely barbed quality; the kiss he blew at Jessica sounded

FIGURE 16 A scruffy and cocky Launcelot Gobbo (Phil Daniels) tries 'confusions' (2.2.35) with his blind father. (1987)

uncomfortably like the spitting that had marked earlier attacks on Shylock.

Whatever the approach taken with Launcelot, whether as clown or friend, would-be insider or defiant outsider, there's no doubt that Launcelot's conversation with Jessica in 3.5, after her elopement with Lorenzo, raises more directly the whole question of her conversion and what we, as an audience, are to think of her. Launcelot's opening lines in 3.5 imply a moral condemnation:

> Yes truly, for look you, the sins of the father are to be laid upon the
> children, therefore (I promise you), I fear you, – I was always plain
> with you, and so now I speak my agitation of the matter: therefore
> be o' good cheer, for truly I think you are damn'd, – there is but one
> hope in it that can do you any good, and that is but a kind of bastard
> hope, neither.

Jessica, as a Jew, is, in this view, always a Jew, always damned,
unless she is 'not the Jew's daughter' (10) in which case she would
be damned by her mother's infidelity and her own bastardy. The
scene was cut entirely in 1936, 1940, 1941, 1942, 1944, 1947, 1953
and 1960, and partially in 1956 and 1965, so that in 1971 J.C.
Trewin found 'the inclusion of a seldom-acted scene for
Launcelot, Jessica, and Lorenzo' *(Birm. Post)* something of a
collector's item. The question for Launcelot becomes: does he
mean to hurt Jessica's feelings by his comments about her
Jewishness? Luscombe's written comments somewhat evade the
issue as he speaks of the references to race as 'an attempt at satire':
'We played his later scene with Jessica as a heavily ironic Bible
class, with Gobbo preaching palpable nonsense for comic effect'
(Luscombe, 1998, 24). In 1997, the Bible class seemed much more
deliberate when Jimmy Chisholm's Launcelot held the Bible for
Jessica to see; in that production, Jessica did not take the
comments seriously and even began tickling Launcelot to make
him stop. But Jessica's light-hearted response to Launcelot soon
changed when, after Launcelot's exit, she turned to see Lorenzo
looking at the Bible, perhaps at the very passage Launcelot Gobbo
had cited – and was horrified.

The 1997 playing of 3.5 also suggested that Lorenzo might be
jealous of Launcelot, not so much of Launcelot as a person – why
would the tall and dark young man worry about the short,
chubby, middle-aged servant? – but of his easy-going relationship
with Jessica. Lorenzo's line, 'I shall grow jealous of you shortly
Launcelot, if you thus get my wife into corners' (26–7), ignoring
the fact that here Jessica had been chasing and tickling Launcelot
rather than vice versa, seemed the key; Dominic Rowan's weary

inflection on 'what a wit-snapper are you' (45) implied that he was tired of Launcelot's ceaseless jokes and perhaps his presence as well. And Chisholm's Launcelot was overpolite in his comments about 'knowing his duty', so that the lines sounded slightly sarcastic.

Although few productions seem to have taken Lorenzo's line seriously enough to make us wonder about the degree of intimacy between Jessica and Launcelot, some earlier productions did create a friendly, if not loving, relationship between these characters. Certainly the Launcelots in Barton's two productions seemed comfortable and easy with Jessica, as if he represented her only friend in Shylock's house. Any potential 'sting' in Launcelot's teasing of Jessica vanished with the music that accompanied that teasing; indeed she even joined in the refrain about raising the price of pork. And in 1971, Jessica kissed Launcelot as he prepared to leave Shylock's house (2.3), first on 'And so farewell', and then hugged and kissed him after his second 'adieu'. She even helped gather all his belongings up into his blanket after he had dropped them. She seemed very tender towards him in 3.5, touching his shoulder gently in a gesture that emphasized Alison Fiske's comment (in a note to me) about their close friendship (Figure 17).

What made the Gobbo in 1971 memorable was not only his relationship to Jessica, but what Irving Wardle termed 'the later career of Launcelot Gobbo whom Peter Geddis converts from a clown into a rather sinister resident madman' (*Times*, 1 Apr). Critic after critic noted this approach, although not always with approval: the reviewer in the *Birmingham Evening Mail* clearly found the change pretentious ('played as a moon-faced comic by Peter Geddis, young Launcelot seemed to run from a music-hall opening to something archetypal in the way of clowns and jesters, as if he came from another play of terribly significant nuances called "Waiting for Godot"') while Harold Hobson, reviewing the production when it transferred to London, spoke of the 'appalling stridency' of Launcelot (*S. Times*). Frank Marcus was even harsher: 'The most jarring, indeed disastrous, interpretation

FIGURE 17 A smiling Jessica (Alison Fiske) tenderly touches Launcelot Gobbo (Peter Geddis). Gobbo, formerly dressed in a striped jumper, now wears his 'new liveries' from Bassanio, including a full-length multi-coloured patchwork coat. (3.5, 1971)

remains the mentally-retarded Launcelot Gobbo (Peter Geddis), who declines into raving lunacy, jangling bells and thoroughly embarrassing everyone' (*S. Telegraph*). While almost everyone noted the performance, only two tried to explain it. Richard David, writing in *Shakespeare Survey*, devoted a third of his review to Gobbo, praised his first appearance and his soliloquy about his conscience as 'more natural' rather than 'deliberately acted out', and tried to recreate what he thought the director might have intended:

> I imagine that the reasoning may have gone like this: court jesters were, historically, often, what we should call harmless lunatics; Gobbo, with his 'voices,' is obviously a schizophrenic; it would be a nice touch to send him right round the bend in the last act.
>
> (*SS*, 165).

But David rejects the idea that Gobbo is a schizophrenic, or even a court jester (tellingly, several other reviewers, including Gareth Lloyd Evans, compared him to the Fool in *King Lear*), and argued that sending Gobbo 'off his head' during Lorenzo and Jessica's moonlight scene was 'unforgivable in this scene of utter relaxation'. Irving Wardle, seeing the production a year later in London, offered a different explanation, noting the 'novelty' of 'a Launcelot Gobbo (Peter Geddis) who loses his wits in his delight at escaping from Shylock and haunts the remainder of the play as a resident madman' (*Times*, 23 Jun 1972).

Whatever the reasoning behind Geddis's striking performance, the playing of Gobbo as something more than a comic raises interesting questions about the character's place in the play. One can see in the various interpretations – from Geddis's madman to Luscombe's outclassed suburbanite – attempts to integrate Launcelot into the play. In 1997 Jimmy Chisholm tried to invade the casket plot in a little pre-show to the second half, where he played around with the three caskets and even managed to open the gold and silver ones. Thus, he created the possibility that someone (i.e. himself) could tip off Bassanio about the lead casket; indeed, during the run of the production, Launcelot became increasingly anxious to share his discovery, and was, during the Bassanio/Portia dialogue before the choosing, pulled upstage, mouth open, by one of the servants.

Paradoxically, the most likely – and the textually supported – way to create a 'later career' for Gobbo has yet to be tried at Stratford. When Lorenzo confronts Launcelot in 3.5, he accuses him of an offstage dalliance: 'the Moor is with child by you Launcelot' (35–6), and Gobbo doesn't deny the charge: 'It is much that the Moor should be more than reason: but if she be less than an honest woman, she is indeed more than I took her for' (37–9). The lines are frequently cut – even in 1971, the only production to list such a character, Portia's Maid, 'a Moor'. (The role was played by Lynn Dearth, but seems to have vanished from the production when, late in the Stratford run, Dearth took over as Nerissa.)

Launcelot Gobbo could have a non-verbal relationship with such a character if directors chose – and although no one has made such a choice so far, the move to supply Launcelot with an inner life as well as external quips might surely lead one day to yet another subplot, Launcelot and the Moor.

4

BELMONT

From Bassanio's first description of the woman he seeks in marriage, Portia and her home in Belmont are inextricably linked; so too are personal and financial considerations, since, as many critics have noted, Bassanio mentions Portia's wealth before he offers the more conventional lover's praise:

> In Belmont is a lady richly left,
> And she is fair, and (fairer than that word),
> Of wondrous virtues.
>
> (1.1.161–3)

But whether Bassanio loves her because she is rich or because she is beautiful – or whether any of the many suitors who throng to Belmont come for money or for love – is not a question that Portia herself can solve. Indeed Portia seems at first curiously limited, as Harley Granville-Barker noted in his Preface to the play: 'Shakespeare can do little enough with Portia while she is still the slave of the caskets; incidentally, the actress must resist the temptation to try and do more. She has this picture of an enchanted princess to present, verse and prose to speak perfectly, and she had better be content with that' (Granville-Barker, 84). This description of her as 'an enchanted princess' is consistent with Barker's opening description of the play as a 'fairy tale', and with a series of allusions to her as a princess who must be rescued: she is, for Bassanio, 'the golden fleece' sought by 'many Jasons' (1.1.170,

172), an allusion echoed by Gratiano after Bassanio successfully chooses the right casket: 'We are the Jasons, we have won the fleece' (3.2.240); and Portia, watching Bassanio survey the caskets, compares him to Alcides (Hercules) 'when he did redeem / The virgin tribute, paid by howling Troy / To the sea-monster' (3.2.55–7). In her mind, Bassanio is the hero come to rescue her, as Hercules rescued Hesione, the Trojan princess offered as a sacrifice.

But increasingly productions have raised more questions about Portia, challenging Granville-Barker's assumptions that the actress should 'resist' the temptation to offer a complicated view. The questions grow primarily out of two scenes, her first appearance in 1.2 and the play's final scene. When Portia first appears, she complains to Nerissa about the suitors by making jokes based on national stereotypes. Later, when the dark-skinned Prince of Morocco fails to win her, she comments after his departure: 'Let all of his complexion choose me so' (2.7.79). While these lines may raise more eyebrows today than they did even fifty years ago, it's still difficult to overlook them in a play so filled with prejudicial stereotyping. As Sinead Cusack (Portia in 1981) puts it, the problem for the actress playing Portia 'is to escape the effect of a spoilt brat maliciously destroying her suitors' (Cusack, 33).

And at the end of the play, back in Belmont after triumphing over Shylock in the court scene, and, as a result, getting the ring she gave Bassanio as recompense for her work, Portia plays an elaborate – and to some tastes, overextended – joke on her husband, first upbraiding him for giving away the ring, then saying that she will sleep with the lawyer to whom he claims to have given it. Is this scene simply a way to lighten the play's atmosphere after the tension of the trial scene, or does Portia's pretence become tedious, perhaps even irritating? Is Portia in this scene, as in her first appearance, likely to appear as the 'spoilt brat' again?

Such questions formed part of Sinead Cusack's preparation for playing Portia in 1981. Her first reading of the part, when she was still a teenager, showed her Portia's 'warmth and humanity, together with wit and a shining intelligence' but then her theatre-going experience had her leaving the theatre 'not liking Portia very much' (Cusack, 29). Her answer to these conflicts became a new question:

> I finally worked out that the great problem for the actress playing the role is to reconcile the girl at home in Belmont early in the play with the one who plays a Daniel come to judgement in the Venetian court. I couldn't understand why Shakespeare makes her unsympathetic in those early scenes – the spoilt little rich girl dismissing suitor after suitor in very witty and derisory fashion. The girl who does that, I thought, is not the woman to deliver the 'quality of mercy' speech.   (Cusack, 29–30)

Cusack's delineation of two Portias, as it were, is echoed in Deborah Findlay's experience of rehearsing the role for the 1987 production. She saw the separation as the transition 'from passive to active state' and the pivotal scene the one in which Bassanio chooses the right casket; 'the first half was Portia bound and the second Portia unleashed'. Indeed, to stress the change, the 'tremendous surge of released energy' (Findlay, 61) that Portia feels once she is free of the burden of the casket test, the production set 3.4, the scene where she announces her plan to go to Venice, in the 'casket room', but with the caskets now being packed away. As Findlay saw it, 'The casket room was no longer of use' (62). Cusack's relief was even more evident in what she describes as 'an unashamedly theatrical moment': 'I look from Bassanio to the caskets and then in joyful abandon I pick up those wretched boxes, which have threatened me for so long, and I fling them violently across the room' (Cusack, 37).

If there is, in effect, not simply one Portia (the fairy-tale princess) but at least two, the question becomes how to give full value to both and yet, at the same time, to connect the woman who jokes, perhaps maliciously, but certainly thoughtlessly, about her suitors, and the woman who dominates the courtroom in

Venice. The earlier Portia is, we may say, the Portia of Belmont, and thus the way in which any given production portrays Belmont becomes an interpretation of Portia. And the choices about Belmont are influenced by a variety of factors.

Perhaps most important is the frequent contrast between Venice and Belmont. One thinks, for example, of Gregory Doran's 1997 production, beginning with a dark and heavy Venice, dimly lit, with suggestions of old brick buildings, black with centuries of dirt and backed by a scrim through which the familiar Venetian emblem, the lion of St Mark, was visible. Belmont was simply, but easily, evoked for scene 2, by flying in a golden arch and by changing the scrim's lighting so that the audience saw, instead of the lion of St Mark, a small Grecian 'temple' on a hill. The stage lights brightened and two women in colourful attire entered, Nerissa in bright green and a restless Portia, a gold-green brocaded wrap over her green dress, with lots of reddish-gold hair pulled back from her strong-featured face. In addition, there were two more female servants, and one male servant, a choice that points up the notion that Belmont tends to be a female society, while Venice is a male society. Indeed, depending on the director's choices, but perhaps also on the theatre's salary resources, the number of Portia's attendants may vary considerably.

While counting servants may seem at first a trivial activity, in fact the number and gender of Portia's attendants is one way to characterize her quickly. The bare minimum (not counting Nerissa, who is far more than just an attendant) would seem to be the two male servants, Balthazar (sent in 3.4 to organize her Venetian adventure) and Stephano (who appears before Portia's return in 5.1 to announce her return). Since the two men could logically be the same, with the first leaving Belmont ahead of Portia and the second returning before her, some productions have conflated the two, although that kind of economy is a much more recent phenomenon. From 1947 to 1960, Portia's entourage ranged from two to six, featuring in 1953 (to the annoyance of one reviewer who found them 'a distraction' (*Birm. Mail*)) three small boys as the casket-holders. The 1960 production gave Portia both Balthazar and Stephano plus six women, three identified as casket attendants and three as singers and/or casket-polishers; a young actress, Diana Rigg, was one of the singers (visible in Figure 23, p. 97). In 1965, the household changed radically, shrinking to Portia, Nerissa and the two men. One could speculate on the economics of the theatre that may have led to such a staff reduction, but perhaps condensing Portia's household serves another purpose by suggesting, almost subliminally, her isolation, and therefore her vulnerability. Dorothy Tutin's 1960 Portia surrounded by six women and two men certainly must have seemed much more 'in command', more assured, than the lonely Portia of John Barton's productions. In 1978, Marjorie Bland was attended only by Nerissa and Balthazar. Barton emphasized Portia's isolation even further when he directed the play again on the main stage in 1981; there, Sinead Cusack's Portia had only Nerissa and a servant (Sara Moore). Though she jokes about the casting of a woman as 'the servant' ('we called her "Betty Balthazar"'), Cusack speculates that Barton 'liked the idea of three girls in the household with no men, leaving them tender and vulnerable, with all those suitors coming at them' (Cusack, 34).

Moreover, the Portia of Barton's two productions found herself in remarkably cheerless physical surroundings. At The Other Place, known for its more stripped-down productions, Portia's worldly possessions seemed to consist of a park bench and a small low table on which the caskets could be placed. When Barton redirected the play for the main house in 1981, Portia did not seem to get any richer – or any more cheerful. In fact, the same wooden bench returned for Portia's first scene, and, Portia wore 'an old raincoat', something that Barton saw as belonging to Portia's father, and which she still wore. Writing after the production, Cusack spoke of Belmont as 'rather a gloomy place, and not very far away in mood and style from Venice', whereas she came to feel that 'There should be something fabulous about Belmont' (Cusack, 40).

The erasing of distinctions between Belmont and Venice grows in part from the twentieth-century tendency to create a unit set which doesn't require a great deal of changing. In the nineteenth century, by contrast, productions such as Sir Henry Irving's created elaborate sets for Venice, including a bridge over a canal, used for Shylock's departure from his house, and, in an interpolated scene, his return after Jessica's elopement. Irving's Belmont was also elaborate, with a formal drawing room for Portia's first appearance, complete with settee, a page, three women attendants and gold-brocaded satin for Portia's gown. But in order to have such sets, Irving also had to rearrange the play, compressing the Belmont scenes so that there weren't too many pauses to change the sets. Still, one of the effects of such staging was to create for the audience the sense that Venice and Belmont should be quite different. Thus, one reviewer of Denis Carey's 1953 production complained that the production did not offer enough difference between a Belmont 'beautiful and gay' and a Venice 'sombre and sad' (*Birm. Mail*).

Though Belmont and Venice increasingly share exactly the same theatrical space, Stratford productions have varied considerably in how they set and light that space. Margaret Webster made both Venice and Belmont picturesque in her 1956 production, framing each setting by 'lifting up and down a gauze curtain to reveal one picture after another' (*FT*). Indeed, Belmont could be evoked while in Venice, as in Bassanio's speech about Portia, when 'light behind a gauze glimmered upon Portia, indeed the fairy-tale Lady of Belmont' (*Birm. Post*). Sometimes that sharing seems to make a thematic comment, most notably in the 1984 production, when the same red fabric covered everything on stage, and when the costumes in Venice were as besequinned and shiny as anything in Belmont; both places were equally full of gaudy display. In 1987, when the same wooden floor, looking like a series of Venetian walkways, served Venice and Belmont, Deborah Findlay's Portia entered just as John Carlisle's Antonio was leaving, the crossing paths of the two characters emphasizing the similarity of their first lines (Portia's lament, 'my little body is aweary of this great world', 1.2.1–2, seems to echo Antonio's 'In sooth I know not why I am so sad', 1.1.1), as well as hinting at the unspoken conflict over Bassanio.

Occasionally, the move from Venice to Belmont, within the same space, can bespeak transformation. The dark stage of 1997 was crowded with merchants inspecting merchandise, two courtesans offering another kind of merchandise, and huge draped objects; after a young man with a list inspected the objects, several were carted off, and the rest remained as backdrop to the first scene, with Antonio's sadness unfolding within a clearly mercantile world. But once the scene became Belmont, Portia's attendants pulled off the wrappings to reveal the extravagant gifts of the wooers: a huge, mounted, glass peacock, an elegant vase, a silver ship, a mirror with an ornate gilt frame (Figure 18). Portia pulled the gift card off each one, handed it to Nerissa to read and thus set up the series of jokes about the suitors. So, although the use of the draped objects as merchandise in Venice and gifts in Belmont reminded us that Portia is herself an object that men hope to buy, this Portia's control of those objects and mocking of the suitors transformed her into a strong, albeit restless, character.

Her first scene, then, can, through costume and setting, as well as through the performance itself, tell us a great deal about Portia, and her attitude towards the situation in which she finds herself. She may be primarily a victim of her father's will, as was the Portia of 1978 and 1981, the John Barton productions. The cover of the 1981 programme is unusual in that it features a melancholy Portia, her arms wrapped around herself as she sits before a background of bare trees, staring at the three small caskets. Everything about that cover tells us of a young and lonely woman, trapped, as she gazes fixedly at the closed boxes that hide her future. In later scenes, Barton highlighted the idea of the trap by having an ornamental rope (with gold, silver and lead strands) placed over Portia's lap as she sat in a chair. The suitors surveyed both her and the caskets, even going so far as to stroke her hair, a familiarity she

FIGURE 18 Portia (Helen Schlesinger) listens to Nerissa (Siân Reeves) describe her suitors. The elaborate picture frame and the silver ship (behind Nerissa) were draped in cloth in scene 1, and then revealed as gifts from the suitors in scene 2. (1.2, 1997)

clearly hated but couldn't escape (Figure 19). Deborah Findlay, playing the role in 1987, also saw Portia as trapped but emphasized 'trapped energy' as she commented on Portia's 'headstrong nature', noting her reference in the first scene to 'a hot temper [18]' (i.e. a passionate temperament) (Findlay, 56, 57). Similarly, in 1997, Helen Schlesinger's energetic striding around the stage and even her obvious resentment of her father – evident in the petulant reference to 'the will of a dead father' (1.2.24–5) and a very perfunctory crossing of herself – suggested energy and potential power.

Portia's power, while in Belmont, is of course related to the casket test, as she waits to see who – if anyone – will choose the correct casket. Staging the casket scenes raises a new set of issues, not least of which is the look of the caskets. Perhaps they are simply small chests, as they were in John Barton's productions.

FIGURE 19 The huge figure of the Prince of Morocco (Terry Wood) strokes Portia's (Sinead Cusack's) hair; she seems powerless to resist. The small caskets are on a wicker table in front of Portia, and draped over her lap (visible hanging from the arm of the chair) is a golden rope, symbolic of her entrapment. (2.7, 1981)

Or, at the other extreme, they may be even larger than Portia herself, as were the 'gold sarcophagus, the silver box, and the leaden effigy' (*Birm. Post*) used in 1971, huge movable structures that actually opened up to reveal figures inside (Figure 20). Sometimes the caskets are carried on, as they were in 1956 and 1960, and then again in 1997, when Nerissa and two servants, each dressed in the appropriate colour, held the caskets. But they can also appear and disappear mechanically, as did the three little

FIGURE 20 Giant caskets dominated the choosing scenes in the 1971 production. Portia (Judi Dench) listens to Arragon (Derek Godfrey) while Nerissa (Polly James) watches. Arragon stands by the silver casket, which featured a large woman's face; to the left is the gold casket, with a sculpted woman's body on it, while towards the centre back is the life-size lead casket, a draped female figure.

Palladian villas covered with matching toaster covers that rose from the front of the stage in 1987 (see Figure 24, p. 102). The ultimate in mechanically operated caskets came in 1984, when the three caskets hung above the stage throughout the performance, each 'vast Chinese jar' (*SS*, 207) on its own long, metal, cantilevered support, to be lowered to the stage floor when needed (Figure 21). Each casket opened to produce a figure – not just a death's head for Morocco, but a full skeleton, and, as in the 1971 production, a full-size model of Portia. At one point in the rehearsal process, the director planned to have Portia's father, or, as he was finally listed in the programme, 'the Ghost of Portia's Father', present at the casket scenes, reading the information on each casket and on the scrolls within; in production, the actor

FIGURE 21 Ultz's set for the 1984 production featured a stage draped with rich red tapestries, two huge pipe organs (one of which is visible) and the caskets resting on platforms that were then lowered for the casket scenes.

(Richard Easton) remained offstage, but still read the lines. Mechanical problems dogged the presentation of the caskets: the Portia effigy nodded when it appeared, sending audiences into sniggering laughter; Morocco's cloak got entangled on the base of a casket, and his efforts to disentangle himself earned a round of applause; and the skeleton in the gold casket rattled badly. The stage manager's reports indicate continuing problems with the gold casket, with stagehands repeatedly having to reset the skeleton, desperately padding it with cushions, but without solving the difficulty.

But while the design and movement of the caskets are clearly matters of importance, the more significant aspect of the first casket scenes is the interaction between Portia and her suitors.

Here too productions have varied considerably, not only in the portrayal of Morocco and Arragon, but in the amount of confidence, or lack of it, with which Portia faces the two men. One problem of course is whether or not Portia knows from the beginning which is the right casket. Most actors have chosen not to know, for the obvious reason that then Portia's interest in the choice is even keener. Sinead Cusack puts the reasoning forcefully:

> We decided early in rehearsal that neither Portia nor Nerissa knew the contents of the caskets, and that Portia's suggestion that Nerissa set a glass of Rhenish wine 'on the contrary casket' [1.2.92] was no more than an inconsequential joke. We also decided that no suitor had yet undergone the ritual of choice. Both decisions made good theatrical sense, heightening the tensions of expectation and highlighting the horrors of both Portia's predicament and that of her unfortunate wooers. (Cusack, 33)

Though the audience, like Portia, does not know the secret of the caskets, it does possess one advantage, namely the knowledge that Bassanio has succeeded in getting the loan from Shylock, and is therefore heading towards Belmont. But although Portia has revealed in 1.2, her interest in the young Venetian (usually with excitement in her voice when she names Bassanio), she cannot know that he will seek her out. So though she may feel trapped by her father's will, she is, to some extent, free to take the first two suitors on their own terms, seeing them as they are.

But who *are* they? What are they like? The stage direction introducing Morocco – '*a tawny Moor all in white, and three or four followers accordingly*' (2.1.0.1–2) – manages to suggest his wealth and to emphasize his race. Though Morocco may be a '*tawny Moor*' and therefore possibly a light-skinned as opposed to a dark-skinned Moor, his white costume will contrast with his skin colour and thus focus us on that colour. So too, his opening line, 'Mislike me not for my complexion', which makes us again look at his colour. Has he experienced social rejection before and is nervous as a result? Or is he trying to shame Portia into appropriate behaviour by indicating that he knows some might 'mislike' him because he's of another race? Perhaps his defence of himself represents a strategic offence, since he offers to cut himself, along with an imagined white rival, 'the fairest creature northward born', so that Portia can see 'whose blood is reddest, his or mine' (4, 7). The mixture of bravado and violence in that offer typifies all of Morocco's speeches; he asserts his sexual prowess, he boasts of his military exploits, and, when reading the inscriptions on the caskets, he scornfully rejects the lead one, saying, 'A golden mind stoops not to shows of dross' (2.7.20), thereby implicitly bragging of his own 'golden mind'. The 1971 production slightly moderated Morocco's military aspect by having him bring Portia a small kitten as a gift. The idea seems to have started with the kitten given to the newlyweds, Judi Dench and Michael Williams, who played Portia and Bassanio. But it remained in the production, occasioning 'animal interest' stories the following year when the new Portia, Susan Fleetwood, held kitten auditions in Newcastle (for the spring tour), and the understated instruction on the property manager's running list, 'Collect kitten from wherever it's lurking, put in cat box PS, hand to Bob Ashby [the new Morocco in 1972] on USP steps.'

Shakespeare gives Morocco two scenes, framing the story of the elopement of Jessica and Lorenzo. Although these two scenes have recently been condensed and played as one – the productions of 1987, 1993 and 1997 all made that choice – such condensation inevitably diminishes Portia's visibility and perhaps even her importance. While the first Morocco scene stresses the character of the suitor, as well as the penalty for making the wrong choice, the second scene involves a very long speech for Morocco (2.7.13–60) as he rereads all of the inscriptions and comments on them. This seemingly daunting speech actually offers a marvellous opportunity for an actor to extend his characterization of Morocco, usually making him more boastful, and often more threatening. Thus, Sinead Cusack described both Morocco and Arragon as circling 'like animals, getting ready to pounce, one might say, upon their pound of flesh' (Cusack, 34), and Deborah Findlay spoke of Morocco's attempt to dominate through 'machismo': 'We felt that Morocco would treat a wife as his property, appropriate her physically, so there was a bit of manhandling in the scene which Portia reacted against' (Findlay, 58, 59). In 1997, Morocco's threatening approach saw him brandishing his scimitar (Portia prudently moved well away), yelling 'for lead, hazard for lead!' (17) so loudly that the three women holding the caskets almost dropped them. Surveying with a leer the attendant holding the silver casket, he asked, 'What says the silver with her *virgin* hue?' (22, my italics). The poor attendant was so flustered that she took the line as a real question and began to stammer out 'Who chooseth me ...' in a piping voice until Morocco sternly cut her off and read the inscription himself. This kind of physical domination – or attempted domination – made possible the reading that Deborah Findlay hoped to convey, namely that her Portia reacted not against Morocco's colour, but against 'being treated as a sexual object' (Findlay, 59); after all, her Morocco insisted on kissing not just her hand, but her entire arm. Still, the final line of 2.7, 'Let all of his complexion choose me so', made Findlay's comment seem like partial rationalization. Indeed, in that same production, one of Portia's servants was a young black man, and he responded both visually and audibly (a muttered sound of disapproval) to Portia's line, thus calling attention to it, and forcing the audience to regard her response as racist. In 1993, the production cut the line completely, as well as many of Portia's references to Shylock as 'Jew' or 'the Jew'.

The racial issue is difficult to avoid, especially since Morocco is one of only three 'Moors' in Shakespeare. The language can sound swaggering and arrogant, but it can also sound 'tremendously passionate and sincere' as in Mark Dignam's 1956 portrayal (*Stage*) or 'dignified', a comment made by several reviewers of Paul Hardwick's 1960 Morocco. Although he too brandished his scimitar uncomfortably close to Portia (Figure 22), he remained 'impressively potent' (*D. Mail*) and even discovered 'dignity in

FIGURE 22 Paul Hardwick's Morocco brandishes his scimitar and Dorothy Tutin's Portia reacts with alarm. (2.7, 1960)

suffering' (*Liv. D. Post*). W.A. Darlington of the *Daily Telegraph* also remarked on Hardwick's 'great dignity' and saw in this Morocco 'a sort of young Othello'. Indeed, the 1993 Morocco, Ray Fearon, went on to play a highly praised Othello just six years later. Increasingly at Stratford, the role has been played not by actors in blackface (and Paul Hardwick earned those glowing reviews in spite of 'a nigger minstrel make-up' as Edmund Gardner put it in the *Stratford-upon-Avon Herald*) but by black actors – and often ones whose other roles suggest their power and attractiveness; Hakeem Kae-Kazim in 1987 was also playing a major role in a new play, *Indigo*, dealing with the British slave trade, and Evroy Deer followed his 1997 Morocco with Ferdinand in *The Tempest*.

While Morocco has frequently been young and virile, Arragon is usually middle-aged, old or even verging on senility. This tendency to play Arragon as non-threatening and highly comic may derive from the fact that he occupies the uncomfortable middle position; the audience has already heard the rules, knows about the inscriptions, and has probably figured out that since the gold casket isn't the right one, the silver one probably isn't either. Thus Arragon can well seem tedious, unless some inventive playing goes on. One approach is to focus not only on Arragon, but on Portia's response to the situation. In 1953, aided by the three pages holding the caskets, one of whom started giggling as Arragon perused the caskets' inscriptions, Peggy Ashcroft's Portia made a 'finger on mouth sign' to quieten the giggler. A more unusual choice came from Helen Schlesinger's Portia (1997), so desperately worried that the tottery Arragon of Colin George might choose correctly that she tried to force him to open the gold casket, knowing as she did so that it wasn't the right one. This Arragon, so close to senility that he needed a posh, mustachioed servant to remind him of the third condition applying to the suitors, took a very long pause after reading the inscription on the gold casket and snapped his fingers as if to signify 'yes, this is the one'. Portia hastily signalled Balthazar to place a stand centre stage and Nerissa to put the casket on it, but finally realized that he wasn't going to take the key she was offering him. Not only did this little bit of inserted detail show us how eager Schlesinger's Portia was to avoid Arragon, but it also made clear that she didn't know which was the right casket and, even with a choice between silver and lead, didn't want to risk Arragon's correct guess.

An earlier version of the elderly Arragon appeared in 1987 when Richard Conway's white-haired Prince sported an elegant blue-and-silver suit, and a slight Spanish accent, and delivered his lines with a maddening slowness. When he asked, 'What says the golden chest?' (2.9.23), and paused, Portia started to read the inscription, just to keep things moving along; but he raised his hand, as if to say 'let me take my turn' with the line, 'ha! let me see'. Similarly, Jonathan Miller's 1970 production at the National Theatre featured Charles Kay as an Arragon so old that he needed help getting on stage, and so senile that he kept dropping sugar lump after sugar lump into his dainty cup of tea, apparently unaware that he had sweetened it. And in 1956, Clive Revill was described variously as a 'handlebar moustached Kensington-accented' prince (*Stage*), 'a latter-day Terry Thomas, only seedier' (*Leam. Spa Cour.*) and a suitor who 'looked like a Velasquez dwarf and talked like a pukkah schoolmaster' (*Oxf. Mail*).

But without a doubt, the most memorable Arragon at Stratford remains the 1960 Prince, who combined youth, effeminacy, hauteur, and shyness. Ian Richardson was in his first season at Stratford, coming there at the age of twenty-five, after drama school and, in 1959, Hamlet at the Birmingham Repertory Theatre. Review after review singles out Richardson's Arragon in a production dominated by Peter O'Toole's Shylock and Dorothy Tutin's Portia. Though David Wainwright in the *Evening News* found the comedy 'overdone' with Richardson as 'a parody Hamlet in sable and silver, reciting his speeches as if laying a foundation stone', most critics were delighted. J.C. Trewin, an indefatigable theatre-goer and perceptive theatre historian, comments:

> nobody had ever seen before a Prince of Arragon like that of Ian Richardson, subtly amusing as an ineffectual Don, ushered in by something that reminded me of my school song, and attended by two new Shakespearian characters, a tutor and a most redoubtable matriarch (Maroussia Frank) who had obviously stepped from the frame of a Goya.   (*Birm. Post*)

The reviewer for the *Birmingham Mail* mentioned Richardson's 'fluting ecclesiastical tones', W.A. Darlington called him 'a mere schoolboy attended by a grim old mother and an assiduous tutor' (*D. Telegraph*), and the *Times* reviewer adds the telling detail that Richardson's 'Spanish decadent ... comes wooing with his mother to hold his hand' (Figure 23). Indeed, the *Guardian* review began with Richardson's performance:

> Judged as pure comedy the show on Tuesday belonged to Ian Richardson whose Prince of Arragon was incontestably conceived in

FIGURE 23 The Prince of Arragon (Ian Richardson) gazes at the silver casket held by one of the three casket attendants. To the left his tutor (Julian Battersby) watches, while his mother (Maroussia Frank), with an elaborate headdress, stands behind him. Portia (Dorothy Tutin) sits to the right; behind her are Stephano (Clifford Rose) and Nerissa (Susan Maryott). More servants gather on the balcony, including, second from right, Diana Rigg (2.9, 1960)

the pure spirit of solemnity made comic by its own portentous caperings. Happiest thoughts of all were the on-stage prompt from the Prince's tutor (an extra character who spoke but two telling words) and the presence of his formidable mother who spoke none at all but nonetheless managed to convey a terrifying matriarchy.

Dressed all in black (the references to 'ecclesiastical tones' may have been prompted by Richardson's costume as well as by his intonations), the young Prince had clearly memorized the conditions imposed on the suitors, but equally clearly hadn't remembered them (hence the prompt from the tutor). And his lengthy speech went on for so long that one of the serving-women actually staggered and fainted near the end, leading to a warning cough from Arragon's mother, a signal to stop the rhetoric and proceed, as Richardson did with, 'well, but to my choice' (2.9.49). Richardson in 1960 and Colin George in 1997 both found a way to make the speech playable, by suggesting men totally mesmerized by their own capacity for generalizing – and both needing a prompt, either from the mother or the servant, to get them back to the caskets.

If the scenes involving Morocco and Arragon tend to focus theatrical interest on the suitors, the focus swings back to Portia with 3.2, the final casket scene. Of course, by now, both the audience and Portia know the truth, and so the question becomes: will Bassanio choose the right casket? For over a century, critics have debated the question of whether Bassanio gets any hints from Portia, pointing to the song (no other suitor gets a song), to the first stanza's rhyming words (*bred, head, nourished*, 63–5) indicating the correct choice (lead), and to Portia's own conflicted speech opening the scene, with its self-interruptions, its hints ('I could teach you / How to choose right', 10–11), and its revealing word-play ('One half of me is yours, the other half yours', 16). Some scholars dismiss the idea, by arguing either for the fairy-tale quality of the play (Granville-Barker asks indignantly, 'Would he [Shakespeare] – how *could* he? – wind up this innocent fairy tale with such a slim trick?', 74) or for Portia's unwillingness to break her oath (Jay Halio's introduction to the Oxford edition, 36). C.L. Barber calls the idea 'one of those busy-body emendations which eliminate the dramatic in seeking to elaborate it' (174), and indeed any kind of signalling would eliminate the audience's suspense about whether Bassanio will figure out the secret, and would also make his long speech seem superfluous. Yet the very existence of Portia's conflicts, her wish to find a way to 'teach' Bassanio, even her extended metaphor comparing Bassanio to young Hercules going to rescue the virgin Hesione from the sea-monster with its assertion, 'I stand for sacrifice' (57), may lead an audience to consider the possibility of a hint. As Harry L. Berger points out, we can't know for sure if Portia offers a hint, intentionally or unintentionally, or if Bassanio gets that hint; nonetheless, says Berger, 'the script encourages us to wonder about, and even to debate, the possibility' (157). And the very fact that the audience does wonder, or can be made to wonder, is part of the play's excitement.

The critical debate – and the audience's questions – are echoed in comments from and the actions of various Portias. In the highly stylized, and highly comic, version staged by Komisarjevsky in 1932, Fabia Drake's Portia remained on stage with Bassanio (rather than watching from above, as she had with the earlier suitors) and Nerissa stressed the rhyming lyrics in the song, especially since R. Eric Lee's Bassanio looked much too interested in the gold casket. And in Jonathan Miller's 1970 production at the National Theatre, the two singers gazed intensely at the lead casket as they sang. But in post-war Stratford productions, there has been no overt hinting or cheating. Sinead Cusack (playing the part in 1981) 'discounted, as too cheap or trite on either Shakespeare's or Portia's part, the idea that the three rhymes invited the fourth rhyme "lead"' (Cusack, 36) and stressed instead Portia's desperation in trying to get through to Bassanio. Deborah Findlay (1987) asks: 'Is the song a clue? I think it has to be.' But she then goes on to argue: 'This is as far as Portia will go to help Bassanio while not cheating her father' (Findlay, 60), a statement that implies the wish to cheat without necessarily following through in an obvious way.

Helen Schlesinger (1997), like many Portias, changed costume for this scene, so that she was now resplendent in a rich salmon-coloured dress, ornamented with a jewelled bodice; her hair, worn up for the scenes with Morocco and Arragon, was now down, suggesting her virgin status. Her earlier impatience and restlessness found full statement in the long speech, and Bassanio's 'Let me choose' sounded particularly heartfelt. But instead of feeling desperate, Schlesinger stressed Portia's wit, picking up Bassanio's line, 'I live upon the rack', and questioning him about it: 'then confess / What treason there is mingled with your love' (3.2.25,

26–7). Bassanio's answer suggested that he understands that they're in a contest and when he came up with 'None but that ugly treason of mistrust / Which makes me fear th'enjoying of my love' (28–9), he smiled at having found a way out and even got applause from Gratiano and his servants. Portia tried again, with the rack image, and Bassanio's 'Confess and love' was a topper for 'confess and live' (35), and again he was applauded as he managed to keep up with Portia's game-playing. Since this production included the sequence, before the second half, of Launcelot Gobbo's seeing what was inside both the gold and silver caskets, it thus shifted the problem of 'cheating' from Portia to Launcelot.

Whatever the game-playing – and whatever the solution to the song (sung by Portia, or by Nerissa or by others on stage, and sometimes by an offstage chorus) – the focus of the scene moves inevitably to Bassanio and his thirty-four lines of deliberation (73–106). Many productions have quietly trimmed the speech, some eliminating the awkward statement about cowards who 'assume but valour's excrement' or the extended metaphor of false beauty where 'crisped snaky golden locks' turn out to cover a 'skull'. But Bassanio's seriousness – and his attempt to think through the issue of appearance and reality – have increasingly become a moment for the actor to reveal something other than the careless playboy of the first scenes. Scott Handy, in the 1997 production, first seen as the tipsy Bassanio nervously asking Antonio for money, and in this scene clearly enjoying his newly rich look (silver-toned coat, silver- and gold-brocaded waistcoat, light trousers), finally became serious; he even tried to explain the 'crisped snaky golden locks' to Gratiano. There was an unexpected moment when, having seemingly worked out the deceptive nature of appearance, he nonetheless paused in front of the gold casket on 'Therefore thou gaudy gold, / Hard food for Midas' (101–2) so long that both the audience and Portia thought he was about to choose that one. Owen Teale (Bassanio in 1993), well described by Russell Jackson as 'earnest, gauche and likable' (*SQ*, 342), was good-looking but no mental star, and he needed the speech to work out the problem. The most physicalized reading of the speech, and indeed of the entire first part of the scene, was in 1987 with Nicholas Farrell's energetic Bassanio, first seen alone on stage with the caskets, pacing back and forth; the actor's image was of a weightlifter who was psyching himself up mentally while also taking lots of breaths to increase his strength. Farrell's Bassanio moved down to the caskets and was about to start talking when Portia rushed in with the scene's first line, 'I pray you tarry'. His eagerness to get going with the test – and perhaps to get it over with as well – turned him into the star athlete with Portia staring at him like the cheerleader with a crush on the school's football captain. Like Handy, he too was impatient with Portia's speech, interrupting her on 'Let me choose' (24). His focus on the caskets – and Portia's upstage position – meant that only the audience saw one of her arms go up in a victory sign, and then the other, as he rejected both the gold and silver caskets (Figure 24).

Once Bassanio makes the right choice, once he and Portia negotiate their first kiss, once past the general embracing and laughing and joking that greets Gratiano's announcement that he has wooed Nerissa, Lorenzo, Jessica and Salerio enter with the news of Antonio's misfortunes and the tone of the scene changes sharply. Productions have emphasized the change in both obvious and subtle ways. Sometimes the clothes of the newly arrived Venetians remind us of that darker world of Venice. Jessica often wears the same dress she appeared in earlier (as in the 1978 and 1981 productions of John Barton), unless the production wants to indicate that she has spent some of the money she took from Shylock on new clothes – or, as in 1987, display her new status not simply with new clothes, but with a crucifix dangling prominently from a chain at her waist. How the other characters respond to Jessica, whom Gratiano with his usual tactlessness refers to as Lorenzo's 'infidel' (217), is significant. Is she welcomed into the group, as in 1981 when Launcelot Gobbo served champagne to everyone on stage? Or, even though Gratiano says to Nerissa,

FIGURE 24 Bassanio (Nicholas Farrell) opens the lead casket, one of the three small Palladian villa reproductions. Portia (Deborah Findlay) waits anxiously upstage centre; on Portia's right are Balthazar (Akim Mokaji) and Gratiano (Geoffrey Freshwater). On her left Nerissa (Pippa Guard) waits anxiously, and behind her are other members of the company who came on as the scene began, and who all joined in the song while Bassanio examined the caskets. (3.2, 1987)

'cheer yond stranger, bid her welcome' (236), does Nerissa ignore his line, as she did in 1987 when she moved upstage to Jessica, then circled behind her without speaking to her at all. But once Salerio spoke of Shylock's hatred, then everyone turned and looked at Jessica; in an effort to make herself less an outsider, she immediately confirmed Shylock's hatred of Antonio (283–9). By contrast, in 1993, when Nerissa did go to Jessica and briefly took her hand, most of Jessica's speech was cut.

The most obvious darkening of the scene comes with Bassanio's reaction to Antonio's letter. He always moves away from Portia to focus on the letter, and must, because of Portia's lines ('There are some shrewd contents in yond same paper / That steals the colour from Bassanio's cheek', 242–3), look startled or upset. But what is he upset about? Is he only worried about Antonio, and Antonio's losses, or is Bassanio starting to recognize his own responsibility for the crisis? Some productions have drastically cut Bassanio's speech, not just his metaphor about the letter as Antonio's body and 'every word in it a gaping wound', but, more crucially, his own self-indictment ('you shall see / How much I was a braggart', 256–7). Nicholas Farrell's Bassanio (1987), using the full text, found in his lines an opportunity for self-assessment and self-condemnation. For him, 'braggart' was only the beginning, and the real truth came with a tone of self-loathing: 'I should then have told you / That I was worse than nothing' (258–9). Later, when he described Antonio as 'the kindest man' (291), his head was bowed, and when Portia asked how much was owed to Shylock, Bassanio's answer, 'For me three thousand ducats' (297), came in a voice which reflected a sense that this was an extraordinarily large amount of money. This Bassanio, whatever his behaviour in the first scenes of the play, could come to the awareness that it was *his* responsibility that Antonio was in real danger; he thus was more than just a callous opportunist using his lover's money and affection, but now a man ready to face the consequences of his actions. Scott Handy, in 1997, stressed his concern with Antonio, even moving away from Portia to rush across the stage to ask Salerio, 'Hath all his ventures fail'd?' (266).

The problem for Portia at this moment is to decide how to cope with a betrothal scene suddenly turned into a deeply personal crisis for Bassanio. The lines suggest that Portia doesn't at first realize the seriousness of the problem, especially when she finds out that Antonio owes Shylock three thousand ducats and replies with 'What no more?', going on to talk about 'the petty debt' (297, 306). The question 'What no more?' seems to realign the balance of power that has shifted back and forth in the scene. From the beginning when Bassanio begged Portia to let him choose, from the agonizing moments for Portia while Bassanio is choosing, from Bassanio's somewhat laboured realization of the fact that he has won, from Portia's handing over of property and self to Bassanio – the scene consistently asks us to see either Portia or Bassanio as 'in charge'. Bassanio seems to take over once he's kissed Portia; he frequently rushes over to greet Lorenzo, Jessica and Salerio as if they are visiting his own house. But the money is still Portia's, and certainly the habit of thinking of herself as wealthy is still hers, hence her question. She may ask the question casually as did Penny Downie (1993), or she may, like Helen Schlesinger (1997), turn the question into a melodramatic 'What?' (with the subtext 'how appalling') and then change her tone on 'no more' to indicate that she was joking. And almost every Portia seems slightly tone-deaf to Bassanio's sense of guilt and shame, whether he has made those feelings visible or not. Her advice to Bassanio, 'Bid your friends welcome, show a merry cheer, – / Since you are dear bought, I will love you dear', inevitably sounds like a callous pun. Thus Portia uses her next line, 'But let me hear the letter of your friend' as a tacit apology – often necessitated by the look of surprise or shock she gets from Bassanio (311–13). Even when the stage is full of people, this moment frequently moves Portia and Bassanio downstage together, to stand apart from the others. Listening to Antonio's letter, filtered through Bassanio's voice, we are immediately reminded of the complicated relationships left in Venice.

Portia's response to the letter may indicate her awareness that this new problem is more than simply financial. Penny Downie (1993) reacted to the line 'since in paying it [the debt], it is impossible I should live' (316–17) by turning her head back to glance at Nerissa, as if acknowledging to her companion that the situation was more important than she had realized. Portia's verbal response 'O love! – dispatch all business and be gone' (321) can be a simple acknowledgement that Bassanio needs to hurry away, as it was for Deborah Findlay (1987). But Frances Tomelty (1984) drew out 'O' in a worried voice, and then, shaking her head, spoke of 'love' with slight irritation, as if recognizing that love can make people behave strangely; she moved towards Bassanio and almost took his hand, but then hesitated to do so. Helen Schlesinger (1997) also used the line as a moment of realization, with her emphasis on 'O' indicating that she had just heard something deeply personal. Then she paused, making the single word 'love' a separate statement, as if acknowledging 'that's the relationship between Antonio and Bassanio'. So 'dispatch all business and be gone' became her quick coping strategy, pretending that everything was acceptable. Both Tomelty and Schlesinger, by emphasizing Portia's sense that this letter was more than just a letter from a friend, underlined what many Shakespeare critics have suggested, namely that Portia's going to Venice is as much to hold on to Bassanio as to save Antonio.

5

SHYLOCK
THE JEW

When Shylock first appears in *The Merchant of Venice*, we are asked to see him first as a money-lender, then as Gobbo's master and then as Jessica's father. But, increasingly, Shylock's Jewishness is emphasized, receiving its most memorable and, at the same time, problematic articulation right in the middle of the play. When Salerio and Solanio move from teasing Shylock about Jessica's elopement to checking on whether Shylock's news about Antonio's bad luck is the same as theirs, the half-hope, half-challenge in Salerio's reference to Antonio and the bond, 'Why I am sure if he forfeit, thou wilt not take his flesh, – what's that good for?' (3.1.45–6), provokes an impassioned response. Shylock bursts into a speech that first attacks Antonio's behaviour ('he hath disgrac'd me, and hind'red me half a million'), then asserts the common bonds of humanity between Jews and Christians ('hath not a Jew hands, organs, dimensions, senses, affections, passions?') and finally turns that assertion into a devastating justification for revenge ('and if you wrong us shall we not revenge? – if we are like you in the rest, we will resemble you in that') (48–9, 53–4, 60–2).

The choices for Shylock are many here. One tradition, going back at least as far as Henry Irving, is to sentimentalize the speech, emphasizing the pathos of 'Hath not a Jew eyes?' and stressing the plea for tolerance, 'if you prick us do we not bleed?' (52–3, 58). Traces of that reading appear in the televised version of Jonathan

Miller's 1970 production, where Laurence Olivier drops his voice and, almost with tears in his eyes, whispers, 'I am a Jew.' At the RSC, the 1993 production actually rearranged the scene so that this speech ended the first half of the production, stressing revenge, but also giving enormous weight to the sense of Shylock as a grieved and misunderstood man.

More often, however, Shylocks find ways to ask for under-standing and simultaneously to insist on revenge. And here the key choices lie not only with Shylock but with the behaviour of Salerio and Solanio. What are they doing to provoke Shylock? Are they just casually insulting as they were in John Barton's two productions, sitting at a round café table, sipping drinks, their very relaxation a provocation to the unhappy Shylock? Or are they openly hostile, even physically attacking Shylock? In 1953, Solanio closed in on Michael Redgrave's Shylock as he taunted him, 'Out upon it, old carrion' (32), and pulled his beard. Alton Kumalo's Solanio tripped Shylock in 1971 and the presence of three Venetian gentlemen in that production (Salerio, Solanio and Salarino) made the Shylock of Emrys James seem even more trapped. The anonymous reviewer in the *Sunday Mercury* ended his comments with a chilling image: 'When all is done and bliss is left, the memory that lingers is the wretched Jew kicked over in the street and lying at the feet of Bassanio's strong young men, two white and one coloured.' In 1987, Antony Sher's Shylock, so often spat upon earlier, was chased on stage by stone-throwing street urchins only to meet up with Salerio and Solanio, the latter using a stick to attack Shylock and also to keep him away (see Figure 13, p. 65). Sher (and, in 1997, Philip Voss, also entering with blood on his face from an offstage attack), was able to be both victim and attacker, using the blood as a visual reminder of what they had suffered. Sher, as reported by Gregory Doran (Solanio), 'with chilling irony ... pushed his bleeding hand into Solanio's face: "If you prick us do we not bleed?"' And Philip Voss slowly moved across to Salerio and Solanio, deliberately smearing the blood from his face on to his hand,

and holding his hand up on 'if you prick us do we not bleed?' (Figure 25).

Such visible physicalization of the verbal attack seems to occur mainly with the obviously foreign or ethnic Shylocks, and a Shylock in nineteenth- or twentieth-century costume often dominates his Venetian tormentors. The three nineteenth-century settings (two by Barton and the touring production by Roger Michell) have placed Salerio and Solanio at a small table, seated, while Shylock stands upstage of the table, controlling the action. David Suchet's Shylock (1981) whipped out his sword-stick and banged it on the table as he said 'To bait fish withal' (47), thus immediately going on the offensive. Patrick Stewart, also standing between the two seated men, actually grabbed Salerio on 'shall we not revenge?' and had to be pulled away from him by Solanio.

And, increasingly, Shylocks have found the lines before this famous speech helpful as a way of motivating Shylock's determination to take revenge. Once again, Olivier provided the key, taking a long pause after he lashed out at Antonio, 'a beggar that was us'd to come so smug upon the mart' (40–1); during that pause, a bell tolled, and when Olivier turned around to look at Salerio and Solanio, his slow phrasing of 'let him look to his bond' carried his new-found awareness that he had a way of getting back not only at Antonio, but also at the entire Christian community that had, as he saw it, robbed him of his daughter. So the thrice-repeated 'let him look to his bond' became for Olivier Shylock's way of realizing that he did indeed have some power. Other Shylocks have used that speech to similar effect; a bell tolled again in 1987 and slowed down the attack of Salerio and Solanio, giving Sher's Shylock a moment in which to discover that he had a way of taking revenge. Philip Voss also took a long pause in the middle of his first 'let him look to his bond' – and in that silence found the crucial linkage between his hatred of Antonio and his pain at Jessica's elopement.

Thus one of the choices an actor must make is how much pain he reveals beneath the obvious anger of the lines. Sometimes the

FIGURE 25 Shylock (Philip Voss), blood visible on his forehead, angrily confronts Solanio (Andrew Maud, left) and Salerio (Andrew Ufondu). (3.1, 1997)

costume, especially a more contemporary one, will signal his distress, as when David Calder's 1993 Shylock tore open his shirt, the gesture revealing a Mogen David on a neck-chain, a sign of his Jewishness hidden beneath his merchant-banker attire. Nigel Terry's Victorian formality (1986) was similarly broken, as he appeared with his coat open and his shirt undone at the collar. Ian McDiarmid, in period costume, used it to similar effect, describing his appearance in Act 3: 'dragging his gown, hair unkempt, half crazed with grief, fury, and exhaustion'. Indeed for McDiarmid, the scene crystallized his grief: 'Something in Solanio's tone brings everything into focus. The Christian plot to steal his daughter was a premeditated act' (McDiarmid, 52). Body language and movement can also convey Shylock's feelings, as with Peter O'Toole in 1960 who tripped over a bench as he entered. So even before Shylock confronts Salerio and Solanio he is already a man tormented by the loss of Jessica.

Still, for most RSC Shylocks, the main thrust of this speech leads to the declaration of revenge. Patrick Stewart (the 1978 Shylock) has written about his difficulty in rehearsal with the 'Hath not a Jew eyes?' speech, primarily because he had to fight off what seemed to him ultimately 'a mistaken notion of what the speech was about: injustice, compassion, racial tolerance, equality and the evils of bad examples'. But once Stewart began, in his words, 'to pay more attention to that word "revenge", appearing in the speech like a recurring major chord', he was able to move from 'a muddled and sentimental bit of humanism to a vigorous justification of revenge by Christian example' (Stewart, 22–3). Most Salerios and Solanios are properly chilled, even frightened, by the threats. They seem happy to be called offstage by Antonio's servant, although the most vicious of the Salads, in the 1987 production, took out their frustration on the hapless Tubal. Gregory Doran reports, 'they beat a hasty retreat, lobbing a final gob of rheum at Tubal as he appeared over the bridge and shrieking the final word "Jew" in angry chorus as they vanished' (Doran, 75). So too did the Salads of 1997 – and the gratuitous ugliness (after all, Tubal has never met these men before) allowed the Shylocks of Sher and Voss a tender moment to wipe off the spittle and comfort Tubal.

Indeed, while the major speech of the scene seems to call forth similar emotions of pain, rage and revenge, although in differing proportions, the last sequence of the scene, between Shylock and Tubal, has received widely different readings, particularly in terms of the relationship between the two men. The usual approach is to see Tubal as Shylock's friend, and indeed the gentleness with which both Sher and Voss treated Tubal indicated such a relationship. David Calder (1993) even greeted his Tubal (Nick Simons) with two kisses. But, in 1978, John Barton introduced a much cooler, more businesslike relationship, seemingly taking the idea from Shylock's complaint, 'and I know not what's spent in the search' (83–4). At that point, Tubal in both of the Barton productions, and also in the 1986 production, laid his bill of expenses on the table; he had clearly gone to look for Jessica at Shylock's request and just as clearly expected that Shylock would pay for the trip. Stewart's Shylock peered at the bill and grudgingly peeled some banknotes off a wad he carried in his pocket (Figure 26). Three years later, the less stingy Shylock played by Suchet carelessly tossed the money at Tubal. The sting came from the readiness with which Tubal produced the bill, as if his motive in coming to see Shylock was only partially for friendship. In these productions, Shylock, having dominated Salerio and Solanio, became almost a victim of Tubal's coolly financial view of the occasion.

But even with the possibility that Tubal is as keen to exploit Shylock as Shylock is to exploit Antonio, the scene ultimately functions to reveal Shylock's inner life as no other moment in the play can do. No matter how angry Shylock is – at Salerio and Solanio, at Antonio and at Jessica – every actor playing the role has recognized the emotional power of Shylock's response to the news that Jessica had, in Genoa, given a ring to buy a monkey: 'Out upon her! – thou torturest me Tubal, – it was my turquoise, I had it of Leah when I was a bachelor: I would not have given it for a wilderness of monkeys' (110–13). Peter O'Toole, laughing in triumph at the news that Antonio was undone, stopped laughing when Tubal mentioned the monkey. For Patrick Stewart, playing a Shylock obsessed with money, the word 'bachelor' was the key: 'That word shatters our image of this man Shylock and we see the man that once was, a bachelor, with all the association of youth, innocence and love that is to come. Shakespeare doesn't need to write a pre-history of Shylock. Those two lines say it all' (Stewart, 23). Both Stewart and Suchet took the lines quietly, after a pause – and then used the pain of betrayal to motivate the decision to pursue Antonio. Tubal's line attempting to console Shylock, 'But Antonio is certainly undone' (114), offered Shylock a way out of the pain caused by Jessica and by her giving away of the ring. Suchet used the pause created by relighting his cigar to come up with the idea of going after Antonio; Stewart puffed at his tiny cigarette.

FIGURE 26 At the café table used frequently in the Venice scenes, Shylock (Patrick Stewart, standing) counts out the money he owes Tubal (Raymond Westwell) for the expenses incurred in searching for Jessica. (3.1, 1978)

Other Shylocks have been more overtly emotional. The promptbook directions for 1971 have Emrys James's Shylock falling to the ground when Tubal reports that Jessica has not been found, beating his head and, by the end of his tirade, wailing and groaning. When Tubal started to speak about Antonio's ill luck, Shylock, still on the floor, crawled over to him. This Shylock also flourished a dagger and, by the end of the scene, had his hands up in the air, practically dancing in triumph. Peter O'Toole, in 1960, an intense and dominating Shylock, was reduced to 'breast-beating, cloak-rending grief on losing Jessica' (*SA Herald*) and a 'tortured and agonised shout' for 'would she were hears'd at my foot, and the ducats in her coffin' (Figure 27). Philip Voss (1997) tore his gown on 'I would my daughter were dead at my foot', an allusion to the Jewish custom of mourning the dead by tearing one's clothes (80–2). Some productions have also, in effect, worked backwards from the line about the ring, focusing on it when Shylock leaves

FIGURE 27 Peter O'Toole's Shylock insists to Clive Swift's Tubal that he has an oath in heaven and will therefore take revenge on Antonio. Shylock's prayer-shawl is partially visible at this moment, emphasizing the importance of his religious commitment. (3.1, 1960)

Jessica in 2.5 (see pp. 38–9) and thus making sure that the audience already knows how important it is for him.

And while the line about the ring is, on the page, the scene's emotional centre, other lines have emerged to reveal Shylock's feelings. Philip Voss made the audience hear Shylock's talk of money as a cover for his real hurt; his inserted pause when he said 'I shall never see my ... gold ... again' (100–1) made clear that he wanted to say 'daughter' but wouldn't. And for at least two other Shylocks the scene has also functioned to show a man's gradually becoming aware of what it means to be a Jew. David Suchet's late nineteenth-century banker, bemoaning his loss – 'the curse never fell upon our nation till now' – provoked a visual rebuke from Tubal who seemed about to speak, when Suchet's Shylock continued, 'I never felt it till now' (77–9) (Cook, 84). David Calder, the twentieth-century Shylock, who, though keeping a Hebrew book in his office, seemed a fully assimilated Venetian, made the same line one of powerful realization. And indeed, Shylock's journey in 1993 was from Venetian to Jew, and it was at this moment that he understood that nothing – not the glass-topped office desk or the computer or even the CD playing Brahms at home – could protect him from anti-Semitism.

So powerful is this scene with its unsparing focus on Shylock that since 1956, every Stratford production has placed the performance interval after this scene.[1] Thus Shylock receives a 'star' curtain, often remaining alone on stage. In 1956, the reviewer for the *Oxford Mail* specifically focused on the 'damped-down menace of Mr. [Emlyn] Williams' uttering, with Shylock's knife lying flat across the palms of his hands, of the injunction, "... at our synagogue Tubal" [120]' as one of 'the most exciting moments of this production'. Stewart (1978) sat at the café table into which he had just stuck a knife to emphasize his implacable decision, 'I will have the heart of him [Antonio] if he forfeit' (116–17). By contrast, David Suchet's Shylock (1981) showed his violent side with Salerio and Solanio, but at the scene's end, sat quietly eating some melon. Ian McDiarmid (1984), who earlier had suffered 'an extraordinary breakdown of wordless grief' (*Times*, 11 Apr), with his head in Tubal's lap, pulled himself together after Tubal left and then solemnly put on his pointed yellow hat, the embarrassing symbol of his difference, here used in a gesture of defiance. Antony Sher (1987) sat on a mooring post, far stage right, swaying slightly as his lips moved in silent prayer; perhaps he was already, in his mind, at the synagogue where he planned to meet Tubal, perhaps he was starting to go crazy with thoughts of revenge. Philip Voss (1997) created an even more elaborate ending, as he moved down centre, rubbing his hand and ring finger, his pain coming out first as whimpers ('oh, oh') and then sobs. He raised his hands to heaven, frozen in a spotlight, and then the lights went out.

Shylock's next scene, the brief 3.3, not only restores whatever control he may have lost in 3.1, but establishes for the audience that Antonio really is in danger. Emrys James's Shylock, taking his cue perhaps from Shylock's line, 'But since I am a dog, beware my fangs' (7), as well as Solanio's reference to a cur, actually barked at Antonio. Sher's Shylock was implacable, progressing from repressed anger to visible hostility; he spat at the manacled Antonio, who looked particularly vulnerable in his white shirt. The gesture provoked Solanio to draw his sword, but nothing could stop this Shylock who then picked up the chain attached to the manacles and jerked it harshly before leaving. Such viciousness was perhaps understandable from the man who had so often been the target of Christians spitting at him. The nineteenth-century setting for both Stewart and Suchet seemed to moderate their behaviour, as did the absence of a gaoler, although the text calls for one. Instead, both in 1978 and 1981, Antonio was not chained, and Solanio (who was dressed in a military-looking jacket throughout) was Antonio's only companion; he was given the first line of the scene, an added 'Shylock', as if he too were begging for mercy for Antonio, and although he was addressed as 'Gaoler', he nonetheless was clearly on Antonio's side. In 1978, after Shylock's exit, and another added 'Shylock' from Alan Cody's Solanio, the latter tore down the poster of Antonio-as-debtor which Shylock had put up at the scene's beginning.

In 1993, David Thacker created yet another variation for the scene when Calder's Shylock confronted Antonio in the office in which the two had first met; again no gaoler escorted Antonio, but only Solanio, and the effect was of a late-night session, with Shylock in shirt-sleeves and yarmulke, Antonio still suave in suit and overcoat. As in the first Shylock/Antonio scene (1.3) Tubal was again present (though he is not there in the text) and Shylock's first line, 'tell not me of mercy', was delivered to Tubal, rather than, as usual, to Antonio. So too was the hope, 'the duke shall grant me justice', but when Shylock insisted 'I'll have my bond, and therefore speak no more', Tubal left, as if to underscore Shylock's isolation. The director added a final appeal from Antonio, who cried out 'Shylock', and then hugged his enemy desperately; Shylock remained unresponsive and left. Shylock's hatred, whether expressed with the overt attacks by James and Sher, the shaming posters of Stewart, the 'playful' tapping of Solanio's cheek by Suchet (promptbook), or by the silence of Calder, is unmistakable, and sets up the major confrontation of the play, the trial scene in Venice.

NOTE

1 Terry Hands's 1971 production at Stratford took the interval after 3.1. However, according to the promptbook for the 1972 London remounting of this same production, the scenes were reordered so that 3.1 was played after 2.8 and the first half ended with the Arragon scene, 2.9.

6

THE TRIAL

The longest scene of *The Merchant of Venice*, 4.1, runs to just over 450 lines, and is almost always referred to as 'the trial scene'. Here the two halves of the plot finally come together, in painful confrontation, and the scene's interest grows from many questions: will Shylock really demand his bond be paid with a pound of Antonio's flesh? will Bassanio arrive with Portia's money in time to save Antonio? how will Antonio behave? what are Portia and Nerissa, last seen planning to come to Venice disguised as young men, up to? will Bassanio and Gratiano, not expecting to see their new wives, recognize them? Those plot questions are complicated further by interpretative choices of directors, actors and designers, all of whose decisions ultimately bear on the central question for the audience: whose side are we on? Or, given the frequently shifting grounds of feeling in this scene, *when* are we on whose side?

In one sense, the most basic questions for the trial scene are where to put it and how many people to bring on stage for it. Economics of space and budget are, of course, part of the equation and, accordingly, the 1978 production in The Other Place set the trial with just a long table and some black wooden chairs, while the 1986 touring production, using a series of trunks and chairs, simply rearranged those. In both of those productions, the number of people on stage was kept to named characters, with Solanio turning into the Gaoler in charge of Antonio. In contrast, the 1956 production used 30 of its 37 actors during this scene: 7 'trial citizens', observers of the proceedings, in addition to 2 gaolers, 4 guards, 2 magnificoes and the potentially foreboding presence of a priest, along with named characters and their servants. Such a fill-the-stage approach continued in the 1960 production although only 22 out of the 36-strong cast appeared on stage; here the presence of 4 magnificoes, a guard and a gaoler, 2 law clerks and 2 attendants, plus a senate officer, but no 'trial citizens', emphasized the solemnity of the occasion (Figure 28). As photographs and the programme reveal, Philip Voss, the RSC's 1997 Shylock, appeared in 1960 as the Senate Officer. Promptbook details make clear his function as the one who kept the court in order, starting with the three knocks of his staff that cleared the way for Shylock's entrance. And while no production after 1960 was ever quite so lavish in terms of filling the stage, other productions have aimed at a similar effect. Indeed, the 1997 production, which had until that point shown a dreary Venice, with a few dark buildings to the side, or one centre stage for Shylock's house, suddenly burst into colour. A huge black arch with the lion of St Mark engraved on it flew in, the screens and backing cloth forming the backdrop turned red, the central set of panels flew open, and the Duke entered, born on a palanquin with an attendant carrying an umbrella behind him. The four bearers wore long red velvet robes, trimmed with white fur while the Duke's resplendent orange-and-gold brocade costume, modelled on portraits of the Doge, both echoed and jarred with the red backdrop. The effect was overwhelming, first for the audience, but even more for Shylock; he seemed almost lost, when he came in, and the Senate Guard had to motion him to his 'corner' of the stage.

Most of the people on stage are, of course, Venetians – and indeed, most productions seek to isolate Shylock by making him the only Jew on stage, although occasionally Tubal will appear as well. Clive Swift's Tubal did not enter the courtroom in 1960 when Peter O'Toole's Shylock did, but slipped in during the general

FIGURE 28 The elegant costumes and elaborate wigs of the 1960 production contrast sharply with the bound and helpless Antonio (Patrick Allen, on floor, centre). From left, Salerio (David Sumner), Solanio (David Buck), Gratiano (Patrick Wymark, in cape), Portia (Dorothy Tutin, hand extended), Bassanio (Denholm Elliott, with money bags in hand), Nerissa (Susan Maryott, seated at desk), Shylock (Peter O'Toole), the Duke of Venice (Tony Church, in pointed cap, above Shylock). Just behind Portia one can see the face of the Officer of the Court, Philip Voss. Shylock's dark costume and Mogen David (here worn as an ornament) set him apart from everyone except, perhaps, the dark-clad Portia. (4.1)

flurry of getting Bellario's letter. But O'Toole's entrance was preceded by crowd noises off stage, and onstage onlookers had to be cleared out of the way, both choices suggesting a hostile environment in which Shylock might almost seem the victim. In 1987, the obstreperous urchins who had constantly harassed Shylock were once again present, but this Shylock was accompanied not only by Tubal but by another (unnamed) Jew; jeering occurred as soon as Shylock appeared, but, supported by his friends, and obsessed with his preparations, Antony Sher seemed impervious. Even when Bassanio spat on him, Shylock simply wiped away the spittle, but didn't retreat. His lack of response made Bassanio seem weak – as well as vicious. The 1981 production offered a stunningly different look after Shylock's entrance, when Solanio (appearing not only as one of Antonio's companions but also as a functionary of the court) served sherry to the Duke, to Antonio and even to a seated Shylock; David Suchet's Shylock waved away such meaningless courtesy.

While a stage crowded with extras and full of brilliant display can seem to overwhelm Shylock and even make him look like a victim, he nonetheless dominates the first part of the scene (until Portia's entrance). Indeed, in 1997, though Philip Voss's Shylock was the only Jew on stage and clearly outnumbered by the Venetians, he also stood out against the brilliant background because of his black costume. The text similarly emphasizes Shylock; he not only has one-third of the first 140 lines, but he gets two long speeches with which to control the stage. Both of these speeches display his power as he asks a question that surely troubles the offstage audience as well as the onstage characters: 'You'll ask me why I rather choose to have / A weight of carrion flesh, than to receive / Three thousand ducats.' We lean forward, waiting, and then, like those on stage, are metaphorically slapped in the face, 'I'll not answer that! / But say it is my humour' (4.1.40–3). The more Shylock senses the frustration of his onstage listeners, the more he continues to spin out examples, delighting in his power to make these people listen to him, even when what they're hearing may seem trivial or offensive. Shylock, perhaps unconsciously rather than consciously, knows that he doesn't have a chance of winning – as the stage picture often makes clear – but he nonetheless will take the opportunity to make the Venetians, especially Antonio, squirm for as long as possible. Patrick Stewart wrote about Shylock's 'hour of triumph' (the phrase suggesting that the victory will be short-lived) and used a telling image: 'The knife will be twisted many times before it enters Antonio's body, and everyone will suffer' (Stewart, 24). David Suchet's Shylock added even further delay to his words by pausing to light his cigar in the middle of his first long speech, just after 'now for your answer' (52), thus offering the possibility of a response and then making everyone wait for him. Shylock's second speech is even more pointedly an attack, as he argues that the Venetians' treatment of slaves is similar to his demand for what is really his. Antony Sher gave that speech contemporary resonance in 1987 when he used the line 'You have among you many a purchas'd slave' (90) as the cue for seizing a black actor (earlier one of Portia's servants, but here just a member of the crowd). Here the spat-upon Shylock now mirrored another kind of prejudice to the Venetians.

The text gives Shylock not only language, to which Antonio must listen, but action, implied by Bassanio's question, 'Why dost thou whet thy knife so earnestly?' Shylock's reply, 'To cut the forfeiture from that bankrupt there', provokes an outburst from Gratiano: 'Not on thy sole: but on thy soul' (121–3). Indeed, in productions without lots of extras, Gratiano functions as a one-man jeering section. Mark Lockyer, in 1993, lost all restraint, and seemed so wild that one started imagining a character who had taken drugs before coming to court; even Bassanio was startled and Salerio and Solanio had to quieten him down. Occasionally Shylock adds other business. Peter O'Toole (1960) tested the sharpness of the knife on a piece of silk brought in by Tubal; he used both the knife and the bond as props with which to repel Gratiano's attacks. Thus, when Gratiano spoke of Shylock's desires as 'wolvish, bloody, starv'd, and ravenous' (138), O'Toole's Shylock took out the bond and tapped it meaningfully, as if reminding Gratiano of the bargain. After cautioning Gratiano, 'Repair thy wit good youth' (141), Shylock then held up the knife, again stressing his power. The actor's physical presence was riveting: 'while the trial rages around him, he sits deliberately sharpening his knife on his shoe; he is intent but quiet, not a movement is demonstrative, yet one can't take one's eyes off him, for all that the Venetians scurry about noisily' (*New States & Nat.*). Antony Sher (1987) took the knife-sharpening even further, setting out a white cloth, a small bowl and a curved dagger on which he spat before sharpening it. So dominant is Shylock that other characters rarely make much of an impression, although in 1997 Scott Handy's Bassanio, trying to pay off the debt, threw all six thousand ducats out on the stage with the delighted smile of a small child who has just saved the day, only to have Shylock's cool rejection undercut this naive gesture.

The next major section of the scene centres on Portia's entrance, and thus the balance of interest (and maybe even of power) shifts from Shylock to Portia. Portia's costume disguises her from those on stage, but not from the audience and here the choice of period may make the designer's task more or less easy. Period costume often features hats for the men, although a reviewer commented acidly that Peggy Ashcroft's 1953 Portia could have adopted 'a more effective masquerade than a long red cloak and a black "ski" cap' (*Bristol E. Post*) (see Figure 31, p. 128). Margaret Johnston in 1956 covered her elegant, upswept curly hairdo with a close-fitting hat, changed her multi-layered gown with its swirling chiffon sleeves for dark robes and added a pair of heavily rimmed spectacles to create a suitably 'legal' look (see Figure 33, p. 132). Janet Suzman's 1965 'lawyer' in her velvet hat with brim could simply sweep her long hair up into the hat (Figure 29). The eighteenth-century setting for the 1960 production allowed Dorothy Tutin to appear without a hat, her hair (or wig) swept back into the same long-haired style, tied at the nape of the neck, that Bassanio wore. Though several reviewers mentioned Dorothy Tutin's diminutive stature – Peter Roberts pointed out that 'she looks so slight a figure, one sympathises with the Duke's astonished question, "Come you from old Bellario?"' (*Plays & P.*) – the designer's choice, 'the plainest of dark suits' (*Stage & TV*), meant that she stood out among the crowd of more sumptuously dressed Venetians (see Figure 28). Productions set in the nineteenth or twentieth century usually present a short-haired Portia, without a hat; such Portias – Sinead Cusack in 1981, Fiona Shaw in 1986, Penny Downie in 1993 – often wear a long-haired wig in the earlier

FIGURE 29 The Officer (William Dysart) holds Antonio (William Squire) as Portia (Janet Suzman) stops Shylock (Eric Porter) from attacking him. Antonio's white shirt and clearly visible cross emphasize his victimization. (4.1, 1965)

scenes and then appear in court with their own short hair (Figure 30).

What Portia does when she enters can signal her bias, or, frequently, her attempt to appear unbiased. In 1997, Helen Schlesinger busied herself with her lawbooks as they were set on a little table. So she was not actually looking at either Shylock or Antonio when she asked, 'Which is the merchant here? and which the Jew?' (170). Then she turned, remaining in her central position upstage, looked first at Shylock, then over at Antonio, then back to Shylock, and then finally asked Antonio, 'Is your name Shylock?' (172). Was she being scrupulously impartial? Or was she trying to make Antonio squirm? Shylock was irritated, correcting her: 'Shylock is *my* name' (my italics). In 1987, Deborah Findlay seemed really not to know, and given the number of people on stage, including at least three Jews, her question made

FIGURE 30 Salerio (David Summer) stands behind Shylock (Nigel Terry) as he listens to Portia (Fiona Shaw) trying to convince Shylock to destroy the bond. The Victorian setting put Shylock and Portia in similar costumes, striped trousers and long frock coats. (4.1, 1986)

sense. A modern-dress production may seem to make the question more difficult, but Penny Downie's Portia gave herself the excuse of looking in her briefcase for her glasses when she asked, 'Which is the merchant here? and which the Jew?', provoking an ironic laugh from Shylock. And when Frances Tomelty asked the same question to Ian McDiarmid and Christopher Ravenscroft in 1984, McDiarmid's Shylock was visibly irritated, hitting the scales and letting out an audible sound of disbelief. Earlier Portias clearly knew who Shylock was: Peggy Ashcroft (1953) came in, hesitated for a moment, bowed to the court and then moved slowly across the stage; then, according to the promptbook, 'halts, seeing Shylock, pause'. And Judi Dench, in 1971, having followed up the initial question by asking Antonio, 'You stand within his danger, do you not?', then moved towards him as he acknowledged, 'Ay, so he says'(176–7), and took his arm, thus silently allying herself with him.

Portia's first major speech must be one dreaded by actors in the same way that they dread Hamlet's 'To be, or not to be' or Jaques's 'All the world's a stage'. For the speech beginning 'The quality of mercy is not strain'd', contains surely the play's most familiar lines. And yet, as review after review makes clear, the speech has increasingly been treated as something other than merely 'a famous speech'. In 1953, the reviewer for the *Birmingham Mail* seemed in two minds about Peggy Ashcroft: 'She made a first-rate barrister with a far more convincing simulation of the masculine habit than we are accustomed to, and she threw away her mercy speech, which used to be regarded as God's gift to an actress, just as though it were the wrapping from a piece of toffee'. But Neville Gaffin in the *Birmingham Gazette* praised Margaret Johnston's 1956 Portia for making 'the "quality of mercy" a legal argument, not merely a weary essay in lyricism'. Susan Fleetwood (taking over as Portia from Judi Dench in 1972) was praised by B.A. Young (*FT*): 'she speaks the line "The quality of mercy is not strained" unusually well and delivers the rest of the speech with a kind of challenging indignation that is a great improvement on the philosophical reflection it usually gets'. John Barton described the speech to his 1981 Portia, Sinead Cusack, as a 'spontaneous outburst triggered by Shylock's aggression to her in the court' (Barton, 87). Patrick Stewart, Barton's Shylock three years earlier, expands the idea:

> when again mercy is proposed Shylock tests this young doctor's quality with a simple 'Why?' Her answer is well known and it is a

good speech, but I am convinced that what makes it remarkable in performance is that it is pure improvisation. Any interpretation that is at all predetermined will turn it into a tract. Portia proposes mercy because her upbringing and nature cannot conceive of any other response to someone in such difficulty. She has never imagined that anyone could ask 'why mercy?' or that such a person could exist. She is invited to justify something which is as natural to her as breathing and it is the shock of that which motivates 'The quality of mercy is not strained,' and we are moved as we hear her articulate her faith, perhaps for the first time.   (Stewart, 25)

Stewart's eloquent account of what Portia is like and how she responds to Shylock may come from his own exploration of the relationship, as well as from comments Barton made in rehearsal. But no matter the source, the notion that Portia might be 'spontaneous' or 'improvisational' when she first confronts Shylock then raises the larger question: is Portia improvising for the rest of the scene or does she already know how she can save Antonio from Shylock's knife?

The text offers both possibilities. Portia's instructions to her servant, asking him to take a letter to her cousin Doctor Bellario and in return to receive both 'notes and garments' (3.4.51), imply that she has already planned to impersonate a lawyer and is seeking his assistance, both with information and with appropriate costume. The letter from Doctor Bellario says that Balthazar, Portia's assumed name, was visiting him when the Duke's appeal for legal expertise reached him, and states directly, 'We turn'd o'er many books together, he is furnished with my opinion...' (4.1.155–6). And Portia claims to know the case in detail, 'I am informed throughly of the cause' (170). Later in the scene, she seems very thoroughly acquainted with laws in Venice that, seemingly, even the Duke has forgotten, namely the decree about the penalties against an alien who seeks the life of a Venetian citizen.

But against these details suggesting that Portia holds all the cards and plays them deliberately is the stretch of text running for

120 lines between Portia's attempt to get Shylock to be merciful and the moment when she finally stops him from attacking Antonio. It is, of course, possible to play these lines, and Portia's questions to Shylock, as an extraordinarily clever set-up. Failing to convince him to show mercy, she then seems to take his side, arguing that the laws of Venice cannot be changed; indeed, Michael Redgrave's Shylock was so delighted when Peggy Ashcroft's Portia made this assertion that he kissed the hem of her robes (Figure 31). By luring Shylock into a repeated insistence on the bond, word for word, Portia could be setting a trap. Thus her question about a surgeon, to 'stop [Antonio's] wounds, lest he do bleed to death' (254), leads Shylock to refuse, ''tis not in the bond'; fifty lines later, she springs the trap when she points out that a drop of blood is also not in the bond. But the same stretch of text lends itself to a very different reading, namely that Portia, having failed with the 'mercy' speech, is now desperately trying to stall for time. She asks about repayment of the principal; she asks to look at the bond; she then urges Shylock to take the money and begs him, 'Take thrice thy money, bid me tear the bond' (230). She asks if a balance (scale) is at hand and then asks for the surgeon, both questions which (if answered in the negative) would produce delay. And she does wait a very long time before she stops Shylock. She lets Antonio say goodbye to Bassanio, she announces formally that Shylock is entitled to his bond, and only at what seems to be the last minute does she say 'Tarry a little' (301). If, one might ask, she really has the answer, and has already figured out the 'not a drop of blood' solution, why not come up with it much sooner, especially before Antonio makes what sounds like a heartfelt goodbye speech to Bassanio?

Motivations for the delay are also numerous. The favourite idea – at least in earlier criticism – is that Portia is trying to teach Shylock a lesson. Sinead Cusack argues that Portia knows 'exactly how to save Antonio', but is actually there 'to save Shylock, to redeem him – she is passionate to do that. She gives him opportunity after opportunity to relent and to exercise his

FIGURE 31 For a moment, Shylock (Michael Redgrave) thinks that Portia (Peggy Ashcroft) is his ally ('A Daniel come to judgment', 4.1.219) and so he kisses her gown; a Clerk (Peter Johnson), the Duke (Philip Morant) and a disguised Nerissa (Marigold Charlesworth) look on. (1953)

humanity' (Cusack, 39). And indeed, in that production, she almost succeeded. Searching for some way to get through to Shylock, she continued to look for an escape (or possibly a delay) by suggesting that Shylock might produce a surgeon 'for charity'. And David Suchet's Shylock, rather than snapping back 'I cannot find it, 'tis not in the bond', took a 'tremendously prolonged pause' (*Times*), as if considering the possibility. Michael Billington noted this 'stunning moment': 'The word "charity" is like a dagger-thrust to his own heart. Suchet pauses, stumbles, and, visibly shaken, goes about his bloody business' (*Guardian*). David Suchet summed up his thinking: 'The real suicidal time for Shylock comes when Portia pleads for charity, not mercy. Shylock knows about charity – by God, he does. He's lived with the lack of it. When she mentions the word "charity" he stops and thinks – and it's the only pause I allowed him – then he says he cannot find it, it is not in the bond. From that moment on he goes for the kill and he knows he's finished as well' (Cook, 85).

Deborah Findlay (1987) actually began her thinking about Portia with the notion that 'Portia is naive enough to come into the trial with only the conviction that she can convince Shylock to be merciful' and thus 'After that fails she is acting on her wits.' She created an alternative explanation for the offstage time that might allow Portia a chance to get legal instructions, arguing that 'Portia herself has not visited ... Bellario; there was no time for that. She had instructed her servant to get the lawyer's garments, and any information that might be of use from Padua, and to meet up with her "at the common ferry"' (Findlay, 63). Findlay's preparatory thoughts also included some of the possibilities mentioned above, including the idea of a Portia who may be suspicious of the Antonio/Bassanio relationship. Findlay notes that Portia 'got more spiky after Bassanio's declaration of love for Antonio' and asks, 'Does it actually cross her mind to let Antonio die?' Given that production's playing of Antonio's homosexual attachment to Bassanio, and of Bassanio's bisexuality (seen when he kissed Antonio in 1.1), Findlay's speculations sound valid. She also raised the notion of a Portia 'caught up in the general blood-lust of the scene' (63). However, she finally came to believe that Portia '*does* have all the alternatives when she comes into the trial' (63) and so controls the scene, trying to educate Shylock, giving him 'as many chances as she can to choose mercy' (64), but finally acting with 'strict impartiality' and following the law utterly. Findlay's term 'spiky' was reflected in reviewers' comments about Portia's seeming 'hard', not just in the court scene but throughout. Michael Billington saw her as 'a tough, gritty, determined girl' and 'a clear-eyed, unsentimental Portia' (*Country L.*).

Yet Findlay's sense that Portia controls the scene is, of course, the way in which an actor playing Portia may need to see the action; the audience, however, may not be thinking about Portia's motives or whether she knows how to stop Shylock. Multiple motives drive the scene and any given production will have to find ways of balancing them. Take, for instance, the 1981 production where the mimed undressing of Antonio after Portia's line, 'Therefore lay bare your bosom' (248) was so detailed that it threatened to upstage the Portia/Shylock interchange; James Fenton describes his own fascinated response to 'the meticulousness with which he [Tom Wilkinson] pocketed a stud or tie-clip, as if reserving it for future use' (*S. Times*). Antonio's goodbye to Bassanio, especially in productions developing a homoerotic relationship, has increasingly come to take centre stage. In 1987, Portia listened to Antonio's goodbye with an expression that suggested her realization that Antonio was now turning himself into a martyr. In 1997, Julian Curry's Antonio, who had hidden his love from Bassanio (but not from the audience) began his goodbye in a relaxed, casual tone, deliberately trying to keep the speech reasonably light. Holding Bassanio's shoulders, he did not reveal his repressed feelings until Bassanio swore he would give up everything to save Antonio; then the two men embraced, a long hug that went on and on, with Antonio's downstage hand stroking Bassanio's back. The hidden intimate relationship was perhaps visible now only because Antonio thought he'd never touch Bassanio again. Shylock's voice dripped with contempt, 'These be the Christian husbands!' (291), clearly implying that there was little to choose between a Christian husband and a homosexual lover, and Antonio finally had to push Bassanio away.

Antonio's sufferings can also be expressed through physical means, as productions experiment with ways to 'prepare' him for Shylock's attack – and the physical restraints emphasize his victimization. In 1953, Solanio held Antonio's right arm, Bassanio his left, as Michael Redgrave's Shylock, holding the knife in both hands, advanced (Figure 32). Anthony Nicholls, in 1956, had his hands bound and his eyes blindfolded, with a priest standing by, chanting prayers in Latin; he then knelt, and the priest held a cross over him, the entire court rose, and Emlyn Williams prepared to strike (Figure 33). In 1960, the properties list includes a 'rack and rest-stand' which may point to the curious vice-like

FIGURE 32 Shylock (Michael Redgrave) stands poised, left of centre, to exact his revenge on Antonio (Harry Andrews), who stands with chest exposed, his right arm held by Solanio (Michael Turner), his left arm by Bassanio (Tony Britton). Gratiano (Robert Shaw) kneels to the far left, while to the far right Salerio (William Peacock) stands with hands on hips. Portia (Peggy Ashcroft) is centre and behind her are the Venetian clerks (Peter Johnson, David O'Brien) and Nerissa (Marigold Charlesworth) in disguise. Up centre, framed by the arch, is the Duke (Philip Morant). (4.1, 1953)

contraption that imprisoned Antonio (see Figure 28, p. 119). In 1965, Antonio was held, arms behind his back, by an officer; the stance emphasized the cross around Antonio's neck (see Figure 29, p. 123). The 1978 production in The Other Place used simple but chilling means: David Bradley's Antonio sat in a plain black, wooden armchair and Solanio (once again acting as an officer of the court) calmly strapped his forearms to the chair, momentarily evoking an image of the electric chair formerly used in US executions (Figure 34). The 1987 production took the 'rack' notion even further, with a wooden yoke to which Antonio's arms were bound. He looked like a man about to be crucified and

FIGURE 33 Antonio (Anthony Nicholls) is both bound and blindfolded, held by an officer. Behind him, Bassanio (Basil Hoskins) has to be restrained; slightly upstage of Antonio are the Clerk of the Court (Leon Eagles) and the Priest (Ronald Wallace). The Duke (George Howe) has risen from his throne, while Nerissa (Prunella Scales) anxiously clasps her hands. Portia (Margaret Johnston), legs wide apart, watches Shylock (Emlyn Williams). Even with knife in hand, Shylock seems a small figure, isolated on stage, and threatened by the crowd behind him. Solanio (Robert Arnold, hand to mouth) and Gratiano (Andrew Faulds, poised to grab his sword) stand behind the barrier. (4.1, 1956)

indeed, during the rehearsal period, the director Bill Alexander had considered 'using a crucifix on wheels to which Antonio is bound to have his flesh chopped out' (production records), perhaps with a ratchet device attached to winch it up. As rehearsals continued, the crucifix/yoke changed slowly; from a device with wheels it became pieces of wood lashed together and set in a hole on stage; manacles for the wrists and ankles which 'click shut' (production records) were specified; later the cross changed to 'just a bar of wood which Antonio slips his arms over like a yoke' and the manacles became sashes.

FIGURE 34 Solanio (Alan Cody, right) straps Antonio (David Bradley) into a plain black chair. (4.1, 1978)

In contrast are stagings where Antonio awaits Shylock without any external restraint. When Emrys James stood behind a seated Tony Church in 1971, and clutched Antonio's bared bosom, the image became simultaneously attack and embrace (Figure 35); Irving Wardle's review of the 1972 London transfer stresses the sexual implications when he describes Church's Antonio: 'he bares his chest for the knife, and all the physical passion inhibited up to that point comes out in a deathly embrace with Shylock,

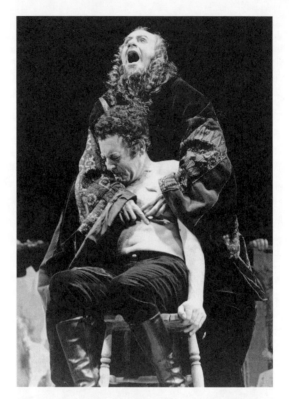

FIGURE 35 Antonio (Tony Church) grips the chair to steady himself while Shylock (Emrys James) feels for Antonio's heart, the knife barely visible beneath his fingers. (4.1, 1971)

whose sweating demented frustration is exactly that of a sexual interruption. Denied consummation with Bassanio, Antonio almost achieves it with Shylock' (*Times*). In 1997, Julian Curry's stripped-to-the-waist Antonio stood with his hands behind his back, rejecting both Bassanio's outstretched hands as well as the possibility of any restraint; he would die, as he had lived, bravely alone. Paul Webster, in the 1986 touring production, went even further. Not only did he brush aside the Gaoler who moved towards him as Shylock said, 'come prepare' (300), but he crossed over to Shylock, unbuttoning his shirt, and then lay down on the trunk in front of Shylock, offering himself.

While Church's Antonio, locked in Shylock's grip, let his face reflect his fear, Clifford Rose, in 1993, expressed his fear with his entire body. The white-haired, dapper Antonio unbuttoned his shirt and moved slowly to the chair David Calder's Shylock placed centre stage for him. Shylock pulled back the shirt so as to expose more of Antonio's chest, and then touched him, near the heart, as if checking the exact spot. While Antonio gripped the chair's arms, Shylock prepared, taking his box to the table, showing the scales to Portia, letting the knife clang on the table. Then, with the clinical precision of a surgeon outlining the operating area, Shylock picked up a blue felt-tip pen and drew a rectangle on Antonio's chest. Antonio averted his head, and Shylock moved back to the table, picking up the knife with a scraping sound that reverberated in the utterly silent courtroom. Antonio began to hyperventilate and shake as Shylock moved towards him with the knife, and finally one of the officers came to hold him still (Figure 36). From the moment Shylock said 'come prepare' until Portia finally interrupted him with 'Tarry a little' took a full two minutes, and the audience, like Antonio, had to go through the scene at the pace set by Shylock.

Perhaps Portia, like the audience, was so riveted by Shylock's preparation that she couldn't intervene any sooner; certainly it was difficult to concentrate on anything other than Calder's calm viciousness and Rose's understandable and embarrassing fear. Other Portias have waited too, notably Deborah Findlay in 1987, watching Antony Sher's Shylock go through an elaborate invented ritual. The production had emphasized Christian anti-Semitism but now, frighteningly, those prejudices seemed almost justified with a Shylock who put on the tallis (prayer-shawl), chanted a Hebrew prayer imploring God, 'Pour out Thy wrath upon the nations that know Thee not', a prayer taken from the Passover Haggadah, and poured some drops of blood on to a white cloth (another echo of the Passover Seder, where drops of wine signify

FIGURE 36 From left, Bassanio (Owen Teale), Gratiano (Mark Lockyer), Salerio (Richard Clothier), Solanio (Tim Hudson), Shylock (David Calder), Antonio (Clifford Rose) and an officer holding Antonio. On Antonio's bared chest Shylock has outlined a rectangle to indicate where he will cut. (4.1, 1993)

the plagues that afflicted the Egyptians); meanwhile the Duke became the icon of Christian religiosity, kneeling and intoning the 'Salve, Regina' prayer. Shylock seemed possessed, a whirling dervish whipping himself up into a murderous frenzy; he tore off Antonio's shirt, and was about to slit his throat when Portia yelled 'Tarry a little'. From Deborah Findlay's perspective – and from the perspective of many in the audience – the ritual was not only 'imposed' but 'almost impossible to sustain'. And, as she pointed out, 'you don't stop someone with a knife by saying "Tarry a little"' (Findlay, 64), even in a loud and desperate voice.

No, indeed, and one thinks back to Peggy Ashcroft's 1953 Portia whose indignation was evident to the *Daily Telegraph* reviewer: 'She hurries across and interposes herself bodily, arms outstretched, between the Jew's knife and the Merchant's breast' (see Figure 32). Such a bold move gives Portia control of the scene again. So too did a seemingly undramatic 'Tarry a little' from Judi Dench's 1971 Portia; she seemed to be reading the bond while Emrys James went through his preparations and her line elicited an audible gasp from Shylock, and, one imagines, from the audience. Richard David objected to the timing in terms of the treatment of Shylock:

> The sudden jolt as Portia's word halts Shylock's knife on the very point of incision was terrific; only I did not catch the word itself and could not immediately recall what it should be. It is, in fact, not 'Stop!' but 'Tarry awhile' ['Tarry a little', in fact] and this surely indicates that Shakespeare intended a much more lingering suspense, with Shylock subjected in reverse to the same sort of slow torture that he has inflicted on Antonio.   (SS, 165)

Frank Marcus, however, read the moment quite differently in the 1972 London transfer: 'Portia's deliberate delay in reversing the judgment on a pedantic point of legality until Shylock's knife literally touches the flesh of the half-naked Antonio can only be put down to sadism on her part', although he then speculated that 'perhaps she feels an instinctive antagonism towards Antonio, suspecting him of being a rival for the love of Bassanio', though he tried to dismiss such a 'disturbing new perspective' (S. Telegraph). The faster Portia speaks, the less likely the audience is to entertain the kinds of thoughts that worried Deborah Findlay, about the cruelty in having 'Antonio spread out like so much meat before delivering the mercy blow'. But, as Findlay realized, 'the company was hooked on the dramatic tension and I was not man enough to cut this away' (64). The question of how long Portia waits before saying 'Tarry a little' is not, therefore, simply the choice of the actor playing Portia. The longer Shylock is allowed to control the moment, the more likely (even to an audience that already knows the play) becomes the possibility of Antonio's death. As Antonio becomes the victim, Shylock, before our eyes, becomes the killer.

One notable exception to Shylock as killer came in 1997 where again the moment of attack was prolonged, but not by his making calm preparations or acting out a ritual intending to excite himself. Philip Voss's Shylock approached Antonio, knife in hand, placed the knife against Antonio's breast and then pulled back, as if he could see that the angle of attack wasn't quite right. He changed his grip on the knife but still couldn't make the cut; then, taking Antonio's breast with his left hand, he was about to cut down with his right hand when Portia finally spoke. The moment became the story of Shylock's inability to kill Antonio. In a discussion with students at the Shakespeare Centre, Philip Voss said that Shylock is obsessed with taking his pound of flesh but has never considered the logistics of doing so and is now having trouble figuring out how actually to cut him.

Once Portia does stop Shylock, Shylock becomes the new victim. Occasionally one looks at Antonio, especially if, like John Carlisle in 1987, he stands paralysed by his escape, clearly disappointed by the fact that he is still alive, or watches to see who will help him dress (Portia in 1971, Bassanio in 1993). But usually Shylock still dominates. Patrick Stewart saw a pragmatic Shylock, one who 'sees the (expected) trap he has walked into, considers for a moment that he will lose, checks the law, and knows at once that he must back off' (Stewart, 27). But such equanimity is rare. Shylock may stand, like Peter O'Toole (1960), in 'amazed helplessness' (*Yorks. Post*) with the line 'Is that the law?' (310). He may still try to attack Antonio, as Antony Sher did in 1987 when, thwarted of his payment by Portia's line, 'He shall have nothing but the penalty' (318), he started to rush at Antonio, knife out, but then stopped. He may actually get as far as Philip Voss, in 1997, who put the knife against Antonio's breast on 'Thou shalt have nothing but the forfeiture' (339) but then, with anguished sounds, turned away and tried to leave – 'I'll stay no longer question' (342) – throwing the knife to the floor. If Voss was defeated at that moment, Emrys James, in 1971, was angry – 'Why then the devil give him good of it' (341) – tearing up the bond. David Suchet (1981), on the same line, picked up his briefcase and started a quiet exit, only to be stopped by Portia's 'Tarry Jew'.

That second 'Tarry', though less dramatic than the one stopping Shylock's attempt on Antonio's life, marks the beginning of Shylock's humiliation. One notes that Portia, who has earlier called Shylock by his name when urging him to take three times the money, or when appealing for a surgeon, now calls him 'Jew' or refers to him as 'the Jew'. Only in 1993 did the production cut a number of these references, so that Portia sounded less prejudiced, less aligned with the vicious taunts of Gratiano; instead of 'Why doth the Jew pause?' (331) she asked 'why do you pause?' and the constant line-ending label, 'at thy peril Jew', or 'Tarry Jew' or 'Art thou contented Jew' (340, 342, 389) simply disappeared. Portia's lines put Shylock into real danger: he is threatened with death and the loss of all his wealth, half to Antonio and the other half to the 'privy coffer of the state' (350), unless he can somehow secure the very mercy he has signally refused to show. The closing line of Portia's speech, 'Down therefore, and beg mercy of the Duke' (359), has always seemed to me to echo her most famous words in a very uncomfortable way. When Portia first appealed to Shylock for mercy, she was emphatic that mercy was 'not strain'd' but instead 'droppeth as the gentle rain from heaven', a metaphor suggesting freely flowing water, not something a desperate man had to kneel and 'beg' for.

The line often sends Shylock to his knees, but with a number of possible readings. The moment may reveal a broken man, as with Peter O'Toole's 'final dreadful collapse to the knees, defeated, humiliated, rocking ... from side to side for the comfort that will not come' (*Yorks. Post*, 13 Apr 1960). Emrys James dropped his knife when Portia advised him, 'beg mercy of the Duke', crossed downstage between Antonio and Portia and knelt; the promptbook's notation, 'kneels, shuffle, shuffle', suggests that the kneeling might have been an acting of submission, rather than the real thing, although Shylock's 'wail' when he heard that all his money was gone and that he would have to convert could then be the moment of true defeat. Antony Sher was already on the floor at this moment, since Antonio, once he realized Shylock wouldn't attack him, grabbed Shylock's robe and pulled him to the floor. Shylock started to crawl up stage, but was stopped by 'Tarry Jew'. As Portia summed up Shylock's predicament, he started to rise, but was then forced to his knees by Bassanio and Gratiano, their attack underscoring the irony of 'beg mercy'. The 1997 production showed a similar attack, this time just from Gratiano who pushed Shylock down on the floor, right on top of all the coins that Bassanio had thrown down (Figure 37). The stage picture made literal Shylock's reference to his wealth as 'the prop / That doth sustain my house' (371–2). Here, the kneeling became Shylock's choice, not a moment of begging mercy, but a gesture of pride, rising to his knees when Antonio crossed over to him so that he was no longer cowering before his enemy. In a strangely parallel gesture, Antonio knelt as he insisted that Shylock 'presently become a Christian' (383), underscoring perhaps the ironic similarity of merchant and Jew.

Other Shylocks have also found ways to make the kneeling a moment of self-assertion rather than merely a sign of defeat. Patrick Stewart's Shylock was abject in his behaviour, appallingly so, bowing, smiling, even grovelling. But, to Stewart, this behaviour was Shylock's way of surviving: 'He howls and whines and he gets back half his fortune' (Stewart, 27). David Suchet was, by contrast, utterly calm and dignified; he crossed down centre, a position that both isolated him from the others and focused the audience on him, and slowly sank to his knees, his face impassive. When Portia asked him 'Art thou contented Jew?' he turned to look at her and she knelt by him; this Shylock, like Philip Voss's later, seemed able to bring the Christians to their knees as well. Both Stewart and Suchet removed the yarmulke that Shylock wore, but Stewart flicked his to the floor with a disdainful gesture (again, playing the submissive convert) while Suchet simply removed his and held on to it, keeping the symbol of his Jewishness with him.

Shylock's final moment is, of course, his exit from the stage, and, as Stewart reminds us, it's a famous moment:

FIGURE 37 Defeated by Portia, Shylock (Philip Voss) kneels to beg for mercy; beneath him are the coins that Bassanio threw down in payment to him. (4.1, 1997)

> Kean apparently went through a startling physical change on his exit. Edwin Booth invented an elaborate and melodramatic mime. Irving was still and tragically defeated, letting out a long sigh as he left; and, recently, Laurence Olivier left his effect for offstage when, after a moment of silence, the audience heard a despairing howl of grief and rage
>
> (Stewart, 27)

– a sound that visibly affected the onstage listeners; the power of the moment is evident in the video version as the camera slowly moves over the shocked faces of Portia, Bassanio, Antonio and the Duke. Like Portia's speech on 'the quality of mercy', Shylock's exit is, for some reviewers, a touchstone moment, and so Eric Johns (*Stage & TV*) regretted that Michael Langham 'had denied this masterly Shylock [Peter O'Toole] a memorable final exit. On the opening night he slipped off at the side of the stage, half-masked by people who were crowding the court.' Still, the preceding moments, described by Richard Findlater, with O'Toole's Shylock 'fainting in court and being surrounded by a pack of baying Venetians who shrink away in shame when Portia comes mutely to his rescue' (*FT*) or his 'unemotional, but whispered "I am content"' (*Plays & P.*) may stand as reference points for a number of interpretative choices, especially the question of whether Shylock has been utterly crushed or not. The 1956 production suggested to Desmond Pratt the offstage continuation of the story, as Emlyn Williams's Shylock, 'rather than accept the terms of the Court that ruin him, leaves us with the knife, which he had hoped to use to take a pound of flesh, clasped against his own heart' (*Yorks. Post*). David Suchet, in contrast, was 'clearly undefeated. When he walks out of the court, it is not to wail and rend his clothing, but to see if there is a boat in the harbour that will take him to Amsterdam, or Hamburg, or one of the Baltic ports. He is, in short, a survivor' (*Jewish Chron.*)

The basic question is how to play the sequence when Antonio agrees to return part of Shylock's money to him, but with the proviso that all of it will eventually come to Lorenzo and Jessica, and that Shylock convert to Christianity (376ff.). In 1987, the text was rearranged and slightly rewritten so that the conversion stipulation came at the end; Antonio, now finally pulling himself together, made clear his notion that conversion was punishment by picking up Shylock's knife and throwing it into the wooden floor just as he said 'presently become a Christian'. Shylock, held in an armlock by both Bassanio and Gratiano, was not released until he said 'I am content' (390), and then as he slowly started to walk up stage, Bassanio grabbed his hand and forced him to make the sign of the cross with it. And everyone spat at him, as they had throughout the entire play. Nothing had changed at all.

Other productions have also read the exit in terms of humiliation. When Nigel Terry's Shylock left the stage (1986), Gratiano picked up Shylock's bag and offered it to him, then ostentatiously dropped it before Shylock could take it, the kind of schoolboy joke revealing Gratiano's immaturity. In 1984, Ian

McDiarmid's Shylock began this sequence on the floor, going from a kneeling posture to being on all fours when told he had to convert. Asked, 'Art thou contented Jew?', he raised himself up to look at Portia at 'I am content', then collapsed when she answered him with 'Clerk, draw a deed of gift'. But then he recovered, standing up, putting on his coat, collecting his scales and his tall pointed hat; his final gesture was to put the hat on a chair and bow to the Duke, possibly as a sign of renouncing his religion, but also leaving behind the oppressive sign of otherness, a hat that McDiarmid described as 'something shaming, more grotesque, like a dunce's cap' (McDiarmid, 49). Irving Wardle spoke of McDiarmid's 'private, businesslike exit – again shutting himself off from the Christian world' (*Times*, 11 Apr). And in 1997, Shylock's final moments seemed to go on forever. Trying to get up after 'I am not well', Philip Voss slipped on the coins. He tried several times to get up, even holding out his right hand to the court guard. On the fourth try he finally made it, staggered up to Nerissa who was standing behind a little table, leaned on the table for support and promised to sign the deed. Then Gratiano snatched the yarmulke from Shylock's head, Shylock's hands came up to cover his head, he screamed, and Bassanio and Gratiano pushed him out of the court.

The effect of such choices is, of course, to make the Christians look not only immature and vindictive, but nasty as well. In contrast, there have occasionally been moments of compassion, as in the 1971 production when Emrys James confessed 'I am not well' and Judi Dench's Portia crossed to him and helped him to stand up. And in 1993, the director David Thacker revised the text so that Shylock remained on stage while the others left. When David Calder's Shylock found that he, like other Shylocks, couldn't easily rise from the floor, he stayed there; Bassanio handed a coat to Antonio, picked up Shylock's knife (a souvenir, perhaps?), which one of the uniformed officers took from him, and left with Antonio; Gratiano's voice could be heard joking about the gallows as Shylock pulled himself up on to the chair, and then, once Gratiano had left, stood up unaided. The promptbook records a three-beat pause, as Shylock stood in a spotlight, just as he did at the end of the first half of the production. He faced the audience, defiant, alive, surviving.

7

BELMONT
REVISITED

hylock's power, even in defeat – or perhaps especially in defeat – is one of Shakespeare's dazzling reversals, as he transforms the villain into the victim. As Shylock increasingly took centre stage, and as nineteenth-century productions became ever more elaborate, thus making set changes more difficult, the text not only got rearranged, with Belmont scenes placed together, but cut. By the mid-nineteenth century, the play sometimes ended with Shylock's exit, as in the production starring Edwin Booth. When Henry Irving began producing the play in 1879, he restored the last act (somewhat cut, both in terms of lyrical speeches and sexual bawdry) – though a year later it vanished again, to reappear in his productions from time to time.

But twentieth-century productions have almost always included Act 5, usually seeing it as a short sequence of love, lyricism, comedy and finally harmony. A review of the 1960 production offers an assessment that seems typical: 'Michael Langham had devised a dancing treatment of the closing scene that had the four lovers flowing about the stage in a gavotte of words and movement' (*E. News*). The opening lines of the final scene, 'The moon shines bright', are, for the twentieth-century lighting designer, an obvious cue. Later in the scene, Lorenzo points to the sky, 'look how the floor of heaven / Is thick inlaid with patens of bright gold' (5.1.58–9), and while the image may literally refer to small golden dishes (such as would be used for Mass), the picture conjures up a starry sky. So powerful is the evocation of lovers in a moonlit night, so hypnotic the repeated 'In such a night', that it may seem churlish to ask 'is Belmont really a place of romance and harmony?' But that question has become one that is asked more and more often, especially at the beginning and end of the play's final scene.

As many critics have noted, most extensively Paul Gaudet (3–14), the lyrical dialogue between Lorenzo and Jessica, with its references to a series of unhappy love relationships, may seem an unusual conversation for two young newlyweds. Why, one might ask, should they be talking about Troilus and Cressida, Pyramus and Thisbe, Dido and Aeneas or, most frighteningly, Medea, the sorceress who helped Jason win the golden fleece and who later, when abandoned by him, murdered their two children? M.M. Mahood, the Cambridge editor of the play, notes that Jessica's reference to 'the enchanted herbs / That did renew old Aeson' (13–14) stresses Medea's healing powers when she made Jason's father young again. But I still find it difficult to escape the more sinister connotations of this reference for Medea later tricked the daughters of Jason's uncle (and enemy) into killing their father by telling them that her magic herbs would restore his youth. Thus, for Jessica to mention Medea is, in part, to raise questions about daughters who betray fathers and about women who destroy men. Perhaps, as Gaudet suggests, she is 'struggling to sustain an increasingly untenable fiction and to rationalize a residual guilt' (10).

Given all the dark undertones to these references, the question for directors and actors then becomes: do the characters choose the references deliberately, perhaps to express some kind of underlying tension in the Lorenzo/Jessica relationship, or do they speak the lines with a sense of light-hearted banter, or are they completely unaware of the darker implications of their words? Most productions have chosen something like the middle option, giving Lorenzo and Jessica a chance to tease each other, but with the knowledge that the teasing is a kind of sexual foreplay, since the two almost always wind up in an embrace later in the scene, as

FIGURE 38 Lorenzo (Basil Hoskins) and Jessica (Yvonne Mitchell) enjoy their Belmont honeymoon in a loving embrace. (5.1, 1953)

suggested by Portia's lines, 'the moon sleeps with Endymion / And would not be awak'd' (109–10) (Figure 38).

The visual cues for the audience are the first sign of the choices made by the director. When Yvonne Mitchell's 1953 Jessica appeared all in white (white brocade dress with white organza sleeves, white velvet slippers) instead of the pale-rust wool dress she had worn in Venice, she was, in effect, signalling to the audience that she was a bride, and a romantic one at that. In 1956 the set and lighting established the romantic mood: 'a cool, green, moonlit garden, with the figures bathed in golden light against a starry night' (*Leam. Spa Cour.*). In 1971, the dominant colour was blue rather than green, but it was still a scene of beauty. 'Timothy O'Brien's sets evoked the gardens of Belmont with a descending shower of metal leaves like a mobile lit in exquisite blues', commented Peter Lewis (*D. Mail*), while Irving Wardle reached for an even more elaborate metaphor: 'Belmont, midnight blue and hung with chains of silver fruit, becomes an image like Joyce's Heaventree' (*Times*, 1 Apr 1971). John Barton's productions, in 1978 and 1981, brought the lovers on dressed in white; even on the bare planks of The Other Place, their status as a romantic, loving couple was clear. And in 1997, after the bright reds and oranges of the Venetian court, the lights came up on a backdrop of pale blue, a small neoclassical temple upstage, a huge moon up centre, and Jessica and Lorenzo gazing at it.

Only occasionally has a director created a less romantic mood – and, fittingly, Bill Alexander's production, in 1987, with its bitter trial scene led to Act 5 opening on Lorenzo and Jessica separated by the width of the stage, each perched on a wooden stump. With such a staging, the allusions to failed love relationships seemed deliberate, a way to indicate the sort of strain that the marriage may be undergoing with Jessica feeling like an outsider in the Christian surroundings of Belmont; the cross that Lorenzo had sent to her by Launcelot Gobbo was clearly visible, hanging from a chain around her waist. The decision to make that symbol part of her attire underlined the extent to which religious feelings were always part of the play's world. In 1997, religious symbols – bibles, neck-chains with a cross – were also present throughout the production, but a close observer might see that though Jessica wore the same dark-grey dress from her Act 3 arrival in Belmont she no longer wore the necklace-cross that had been so visible then. One wondered if she was now comfortable enough not to have to 'prove' herself or had given up under the strain of Launcelot's questions? Here the lines ('In such a night') seemed moderately jokey, although when Jessica said 'Stealing her soul with many vows of faith, / And ne'er a true one' (19–20), she looked down at her hand and her wedding ring; the look may have been merely to check that the ring was still there, a talisman against broken vows, but it still signified underlying stress.

Jessica's last line in this scene of just over 300 lines comes at less than a third of the way through: 'I am never merry when I hear sweet music' (69). That line has, as Jay Halio notes, 'encouraged some modern directors to interpret her role and her reaction to events in a negative or emotionally disturbed fashion, especially in this scene' (Halio, 216) and he cites particularly Jonathan Miller's 1970 production at the National Theatre. The 1999 National Theatre production, directed by Trevor Nunn, actually had Jessica break down in tears at this line, perhaps thinking back to the song she and Shylock had sung together in an earlier scene. RSC productions have not, to my knowledge, presented a tearful Jessica, but they have occasionally hinted at the possibility that she is less than happy in her new life and new world. That revelation normally comes at the very end of the play, but before those closing moments Jessica is a silent watcher of the unfolding comic spectacle.

That comedy lies, of course, in the sequence usually called 'the rings', namely Portia and Nerissa's reactions to finding out that their husbands no longer wear the rings that the women had given them earlier. Portia, as the lawyer, asks for Bassanio's ring after Shylock's exit, and though Bassanio refuses to give away his ring, Antonio's insistence prevails: 'Let his deservings and my love withal / Be valued 'gainst your wife's commandement' (4.1.446–7). The more obviously a production has stressed either Antonio's love for Bassanio, throughout the play, or Portia's anxiety about Bassanio's relationship to Antonio (especially in the playing of the trial scene), the more the audience will hear the power struggle in that line, and be aware of 'the rival lovers', Portia and Antonio, each trying to keep Bassanio's love (Hyman, 109–16).

Even without an implicit power struggle at the end of the trial scene, Portia's decision to tease Bassanio about the ring can stem from the actor's choice of response when Gratiano rushes after the 'lawyers' with Bassanio's ring, although only a few Portias have emphasized the moment. Susan Fleetwood (taking over as Portia in 1972) gazed at the ring unhappily, indicating her disappointment with a line that seems to refer to the invitation to dinner, but actually sounded like Portia's stunned reaction to getting the ring after all: 'That cannot be'. She then covered her feelings with an obvious lie, 'His ring I do accept most thankfully' (4.2.8–9). Deborah Findlay's 1987 Portia was a bit surprised, but not overly so, given her clear sense that she had already seen Bassanio's behaviour at the trial as revealing a deep attachment to Antonio (Findlay, 65). In 1997, the scene looked dark and sound effects suggested that rain was about to fall; Helen Schlesinger (1997), like Susan Fleetwood, used 'That cannot be' to show that she was disappointed in getting the ring.

But whatever the motivation for Portia – and Nerissa – the actual playing of 5.1 usually stresses the gaiety of the occasion, the humour of the situation, and the reunion of the couples. John Barton's stagings in 1978 and 1981 had servants bringing out white floral garlands for everyone to wear, and champagne to sip, the latter touch especially appropriate in the late nineteenth-century setting. The embraces as the couples meet are often fairly quick, since both Portia and Nerissa know that they're about to tease their husbands. The quarrel first begins with Gratiano and Nerissa, sometimes literally erupting upstage as it did in 1987 when Nerissa gave Gratiano a slap that knocked him backwards towards the centre of the stage where Portia was talking with Antonio and Bassanio. In 1997, the slap occurred downstage and Gratiano reeled upstage. But the audience knows that Nerissa is acting, rather than feeling the anger – and similarly knows that Portia's inquiry 'what's the matter?' (5.1.146) is not a real question but a fake one; Helen Schlesinger asked it in an overly sweet voice. The real humour in the scene comes from Bassanio's attempts to look innocent and uninvolved; he may, like Tony Britton in 1953, 'smile weakly' (promptbook) when Portia says, 'I gave my love a ring, and made him swear / Never to part with it, and here he stands' (170–1). Frequently he tries to hide his left hand, and alert directors thus place him downstage left so that the audience can see what he's doing. Modern dress makes the moment easy, as when Owen Teale in 1993 simply put his left hand in his suit pocket, trying to look totally confident as Portia praises Bassanio's constancy. Period costume makes an actor work a bit harder, with Scott Handy (in 1997) getting a trapped look on his face and then, desperately, trying to scrunch his hand up inside his sleeve.

While Gratiano keeps spluttering angrily and helplessly and Bassanio tries to play innocent (often managing only to look hapless), Portia dominates the scene. As she moves, Bassanio chases her, and her references to the ring allow her to emphasize the verbal repetition with physical repetition; both in 1993 and 1997, the upstage/downstage chase was initiated by Portia. If she's really playing outrage, she may even try to leave, as Fiona Shaw did in the 1986 touring production. Bassanio's attempts to excuse himself may, or may not, suggest where the real answer lies – namely with telling the truth and implicating Antonio. Nicholas Farrell, in 1987, did cast a quick glance at Antonio, as if thinking for a moment that he might get some help from him. Patrick Allen's Antonio, in 1960, tried to interrupt the Bassanio/Portia quarrel at several moments, first when Bassanio defends himself with an oblique reference, 'If you did know to whom I gave the ring', and then a few lines later, 'You would abate the strength of your displeasure' (5.1.194, 198), but Dorothy Tutin's Portia took no notice. Finally, as Bassanio swears to Portia, 'I never more will break an oath with thee' (248), Allen moved to stand between Portia and Bassanio, and, putting his hand on Bassanio's shoulder, offered his pledge.

The 1997 production created a similar stage picture, thus emphasizing that the quarrel is not just about the rings but about Antonio and his relationship to Bassanio. Scott Handy's Bassanio knelt stage right (on the same coins that he had thrown down to pay Shylock), and Portia stood stage left, with Antonio upstage between them. By recreating the stage picture from the trial, with Antonio now in the centre, the production essentially made the audience read the scene as the 'trial of Bassanio'. When Julian Curry came downstage to promise that Bassanio would 'never more break faith advisedly' (253), he knew what he was really saying – namely that he would never again ask Bassanio to value their relationship more highly than the marriage; he kissed Portia's hands, a gesture that seemed to make her *his* sovereign, as well as Bassanio's. John Carlisle in 1987, whose Antonio was even more desirous of possessing Bassanio, also underlined the moment as one in which he resigned control to Portia; moving downstage with her, Antonio was, for that moment, finally part of a couple – with Portia – but only so that he could then remove himself from his love for Bassanio and Bassanio's love for Portia.

The moment in which Antonio promises never to interfere again has increasingly become the centre of the scene, often highlighted in its quiet resignation by much physical by-play, especially between Gratiano and Nerissa. And once the truth is revealed, sometimes Portia joins in; she may engage in over-dramatic play-acting, as in 1993 when Penny Downie knelt with extravagant 'shame' to ask Bassanio to forgive her: 'pardon me Bassanio, / For by this ring the doctor lay with me' (258–9). Deborah Findlay saw herself playing 'the wronged wife' for most of the scene, and believed that she was teaching both Bassanio and Antonio a lesson; still, when Bassanio recognized the ring as being the one he gave the lawyer, and Portia chimed in with 'I had it of him', Findlay felt that here Portia 'couldn't resist the wickedly funny pay-off' (Findlay, 66).

The general cheerfulness of the final moments in the text – the misunderstandings between the couples cleared up, a letter handed over to Antonio telling him his ships have returned, and the deed of gift given to Lorenzo – used to signal a 'happy ending' to the play. But just as productions have, though tentatively, begun to question Lorenzo and Jessica's happiness at the beginning of the scene, so too – and even more noticeably – have some ended the play with images that suggest disquieting realities. One reality is that Antonio is alone, not part of a pair, and even taking the three sets of lovers off sequentially, and leaving Antonio to walk off stage on his own, as happened in 1965, will make that point. So, too, did the 1960 production, where the three couples left the stage, but Antonio remained seated, up centre stage. The 1971 production similarly left Antonio alone on stage, wearing black, 'caught in a narrow spotlight in a solitariness that somehow recalled the loneliness of Shylock's exit at the end of the preceding scene' (Smallwood, 193). And the sound cue in 1971, the blowing of the shofar, the strangely melancholy sound associated with the Jewish High Holy Days, also reminded the audience of the other lonely, isolated figure, the one who is mentioned only as 'the rich Jew'. The influence of the Jonathan Miller production in 1970 seems clear, although that production left not Antonio, but Jessica alone at the end, holding the 'deed of gift', as an offstage voice chanted the Kaddish, the Hebrew prayer traditionally recited in memory of those who have died. A powerful variation on the isolation of Jessica came in the 1986 touring production. Appalled by hearing that she and Lorenzo were to inherit all of Shylock's wealth at his death, Rachel Joyce's Jessica dropped the deed of gift and ran off stage, with Lorenzo offering his line, 'Fair ladies, you drop manna In the way / Of starved people' (294–5), in an apologetic, covering-up, tone, and then rushing out after Jessica.

Given the emphasis on Antonio and on Jessica that various directors have found, it's not surprising that one of the most stunning endings to the play – and, certainly, in my viewing, the most distressing – managed to include both Antonio and Jessica. In 1987, Portia and Bassanio left first, followed by Gratiano and Nerissa, so eager for bed that they were already touching each other's bodies. Lorenzo and Jessica also left, moving upstage, with Lorenzo going first. Then Jessica suddenly turned back, looking for the little cross that she had worn on her belt. She knelt to retrieve it, but Antonio, left alone on stage, got to it first. He picked it up, and held it out to her – but also out of reach. The Jewish woman reached up for the symbol that had so oppressed her father, held by the Christian homosexual who would never be able to express that love again to Bassanio. Deliberately he withheld the little cross, as if to taunt her with her 'otherness' – both like and unlike his. John Pitcher summed up the ending in terms of its sexual and religious politics, noting that in this world, 'Christian males stay on top'. Thus, Antonio was seen 'mastering for a moment a victim who is still nothing but a Jew and a woman. And then there is darkness' (*TLS*).

Such disturbing images are a powerful way of ending the play, so that warmer choices come almost as a surprise. In Barton's 1978 production, everyone sat in a circle around the bare wooden stage, a visual emblem of harmony and reconciliation, with the white floral garlands emphasizing the happiness of that world. Robert Smallwood describes the last moments, after Gratiano and Nerissa, and Lorenzo and Jessica have left: 'Antonio refilled three glasses, drank a final toast to Portia and Bassanio, and then walked briskly from the stage, leaving them to make their departure slowly, hand in hand, as the sound of the dawn chorus of birds began' (Smallwood, 193). On the main stage, three years later, Barton's ending was similar; everyone was in white, and even Launcelot Gobbo seemed to have acquired a girlfriend in 'Betty Balthazar' (Figure 39). Both Launcelot Gobbo and Nerissa strummed guitars, and Portia and Bassanio remained on stage, gazing at each other, finally alone together; offstage the song 'Tell me where is fancy bred?' could be heard in the distance. The Barton influence could be seen three years later in the 1984 John Caird production when after a Portia/Bassanio kiss, Portia offered her hand to Antonio, so that the threesome left the stage together. Robert Smallwood found the exit rather more uncomfortable than harmonious, suggesting the possibility that Antonio might become a long-term visitor in the household (Smallwood, 194).

Ending with a tableau, as lights fade, allows for a number of possible readings, often blending feelings of togetherness and isolation. In 1993, for instance, Jessica and Lorenzo left first, then Nerissa and Gratiano, and finally Bassanio and Portia turned to go.

FIGURE 39 The white costumes for everyone in the final scene imply a sense of rejoicing. From left, Bassanio (Jonathan Hyde), Portia (Sinead Cusack), Launcelot Gobbo (Rob Edwards), Servant (Sara Moore), Lorenzo (Michael Siberry), Antonio (Tom Wilkinson, slightly hidden), Jessica (Judy Buxton), Nerissa (Corinna Seddon), Gratiano (Arthur Kohn). Jessica's face seems sad, even as Lorenzo receives the deed of gift. (5.1, 1981)

Bassanio shook Antonio's hand before leading Portia upstage, so the audience saw a moment of inclusion for Antonio, before he was left alone, holding his elegant cane and the letter telling him about his ships. A similar tableau ended the 1997 production, although in this case all the couples remained onstage. Gratiano and Nerissa embraced, as did Lorenzo and Jessica. Portia stood between Antonio and Bassanio, and for a moment held hands with both men, again including Antonio. Then she and Bassanio moved up centre slightly and into an embrace. Antonio took off his hat, looked at the letter and smiled, seemingly content to be there, alone and yet surrounded, and with his wealth restored. The 1956 ending positioned Antonio, still in black, to one side, while upstage the three couples embraced (Figure 40) but his face

FIGURE 40 At the close of the 1956 production, Antonio (Anthony Nicholls) remains alone, while behind him are Jessica and Lorenzo (Jeannette Sterke, David William), Bassanio and Portia (Basil Hoskins, Margaret Johnston), and Nerissa and Gratiano (Prunella Scales, Andrew Faulds).

seemed grimly set, reflecting his awareness of his present – and future – loneliness.

An audience can feel both comforted and troubled by such an ending, and perhaps the blend of feelings reflects the balance of the play. Even though Shakespeare has kept Shylock offstage for the last act, perhaps he can never disappear fully from the audience's minds. Ending with Antonio's isolation – or with Jessica's – reminds us of the man they are bound to, the man whose intensity of feeling pervades the play. And, as the curtain call ritual indicates, Shylock's power remains. Since most curtain calls begin with the less important roles and bring on the stars at the end, it's noticeable that Shylock is usually the last to appear. The 1947 and 1971 productions were an exception, giving the 'star' curtain call to Portia and Bassanio (Beatrix Lehmann and Laurence Payne, Judi Dench and Michael Williams), with Shylock (John Ruddock, Emrys James) just preceding. Still in 1971, after a complete company call, James then came out for a solo bow and called on the rest of the company; the last solo bow went, however, to Judi Dench, followed by a complete company call. More familiar is the version from 1965, with Bassanio and Antonio (Peter McEnery and William Squire), followed by Portia alone (Janet Suzman) and then Shylock (Eric Porter). After a company call, Porter then took a solo bow and called on Janet Suzman to join him. A similar effect occurred in 1984 when Portia and Shylock (Frances Tomelty and Ian McDiarmid) appeared from opposite sides of the stage to share the final call, or in 1987 when Antony Sher's Shylock took the final call but then shared a separate call with Deborah Findlay's Portia; so too did Penny Downie and David Calder in 1993, and Helen Schlesinger and Philip Voss in 1997. The shared curtain call for Portia and Shylock (often with special bows to each other or with joined hands) seems a moment of harmony, achievable only outside the confines of the script but still within the theatrical moment, as these two characters acknowledge each other's enduring strength.

PRODUCTION CREDITS AND CAST LISTS

Programmes supply production credits and cast lists; in every case the listing is the announced one for the first performance. The card catalogue of the Shakespeare Centre Library and its production archives provide the incidental details, such as press night.

1947

Director	Michael Benthall
Scenery and costumes	Sophie Fedorovitch
Music	Brian Easdale
ANTONIO	Walter Hudd
SALARINO	John Warner
SOLANIO	Lennard Pearce
BASSANIO	Laurence Payne
LORENZO	Donald Sinden
GRATIANO	Myles Eason
PORTIA	Beatrix Lehmann
NERISSA	Helen Burns
BALTHAZAR	Joss Ackland
STEPHANO	Maxwell Jackson
SHYLOCK	John Ruddock
PRINCE OF MOROCCO	Paul Stephenson
LAUNCELOT GOBBO	Dudley Jones
OLD GOBBO	Antony Groser
LEONARDO	Tony Maxwell
JESSICA	Joy Parker
PRINCE OF ARRAGON	John Harrison
TUBAL	William March
DUKE OF VENICE	William Avenell

MAGNIFICOES, MASQUERS, ATTENDANTS:
George Cooper, Elizabeth Ewbank, Margaret Godwin, Lois Johnson,
Pamela Leatherland, Joanna Mackie, Diana Mahony, John Mayes,
John Randall, Richard Renny, Irene Sutcliffe, Beryl Wright

Number in company	31
Press night	11 July 1947
Production revived	19 April 1948, with Robert Helpmann as Shylock

1953

Director	Denis Carey
Scenery and costumes	Hutchinson Scott
Lighting	Peter Streuli
Music	Julian Slade

SINGER	Denys Graham
ANTONIO	Harry Andrews
SALERIO	William Peacock
SOLANIO	Michael Turner
BASSANIO	Tony Britton
LORENZO	Basil Hoskins
GRATIANO	Robert Shaw
PORTIA	Peggy Ashcroft
NERISSA	Marigold Charlesworth
BALTHAZAR	Peter Duguid
STEPHANO	Richard Martin
SHYLOCK	Michael Redgrave
PRINCE OF MOROCCO	John Bushelle
LAUNCELOT GOBBO	Donald Pleasance
OLD GOBBO	Noel Howlett
LEONARDO	George Hart
JESSICA	Yvonne Mitchell
PRINCE OF ARRAGON	Powys Thomas
SERVANT TO ANTONIO	Raymond Sherry
TUBAL	Mervyn Blake
DUKE OF VENICE	Philip Morant
GAOLER	David King
PAGES	Anthony Adams, James Morris, Robert Scroggins

ATTENDANTS TO MOROCCO AND ARRAGON, LADIES
ATTENDING ON PORTIA, MASQUERS, MAGNIFICOES OF
VENICE AND OFFICERS OF THE COURT OF JUSTICE:
Diana Chadwick, Dennis Clinton, James Culliford, Nigel Davenport,
John Glendinning, Charles Gray, Charles Howard, Peter Johnson,
Gareth Jones, Bernard Kay, John Kilby, Cavan Malone, David O'Brien,
John Roberts, Mary Watson, Jerome Willis, Jean Wilson

Number in company	42
Press night	17 March 1953

1956

Director	Margaret Webster
Scenery and costumes	Alan Tagg
Lighting	Peter Streuli
Music	Leslie Bridgewater

ANTONIO	Anthony Nicholls
SALERIO	Emrys James
SOLANIO	Robert Arnold
BASSANIO	Basil Hoskins
LORENZO	David William
GRATIANO	Andrew Faulds
PORTIA	Margaret Johnston
NERISSA	Prunella Scales
PAGE TO PORTIA	Christopher Warby
BALTHAZAR	George Little
STEPHANO	Paul Vieyra
SHYLOCK	Emlyn Williams
PRINCE OF MOROCCO	Mark Dignam
LAUNCELOT GOBBO	John Garley
OLD GOBBO	George Howe
LEONARDO	John Southworth
JESSICA	Jeannette Sterke
PRINCE OF ARRAGON	Clive Revill
SERVANT TO ANTONIO	Alan Haywood
TUBAL	Ron Haddrick
SINGER	Rex Robinson
DUKE OF VENICE	George Howe
CLERK OF THE COURT	Leon Eagles

MAGNIFICOES OF VENICE, OFFICERS, ATTENDANTS ON PORTIA, MOROCCO AND ARRAGON, AND CITIZENS OF VENICE: Thane Bettany, Stephanie Bidmead, Antony Brown, June Brown, Peter Cellier, Gordon Gardner, John MacGregor, Brian Madison, Virginia Maskell, Derek Mayhew, Peter Palmer, John Scott, Michael Tate, Ronald Wallace, Barry Warren, Greta Watson

Number in company	38
Press night	17 April 1956

1960

Director	Michael Langham
Scenery and costumes	Desmond Heeley
Lighting	Maurice Daniels
Music	Cedric Thorpe Davies

ANTONIO	Patrick Allen
SALERIO	David Sumner
SOLANIO	David Buck
BASSANIO	Denholm Elliott
LORENZO	Ian Holm
GRATIANO	Patrick Wymark
PORTIA	Dorothy Tutin
NERISSA	Susan Maryott
BALTHAZAR	William Wallis
STEPHANO	Clifford Rose
SHYLOCK	Peter O'Toole
PRINCE OF MOROCCO	Paul Hardwick
LAUNCELOT GOBBO	Dinsdale Landen
OLD GOBBO	Jack MacGowran
LEONARDO	Don Webster
JESSICA	Frances Cuka
PRINCE OF ARRAGON	Ian Richardson
HIS MOTHER	Maroussia Frank
HIS TUTOR	Julian Battersby
SERVANT TO ANTONIO	Roger Bizley
TUBAL	Clive Swift
DUKE OF VENICE	Tony Church

LADIES, SERVANTS, ATTENDANTS, OFFICERS:
Barbara Barnett, Julian Battersby, Walter Brown, Christopher Cruise, Gloria Dolskie, Roy Dotrice, Donald Douglas, Mavis Edwards, Wendy Gifford, James Kerry, Mandy Miller, Diana Rigg, Dave Thomas, Stephen Thorne, Philip Voss

Number in company	37
Press night	12 April 1960

1965

Director	Clifford Williams
Designer	Ralph Koltai
Costumes	Nadine Baylis
Lighting	John Bradley
Music	Guy Woolfenden

ANTONIO	William Squire [Brewster Mason on press night]
SALERIO	Peter Geddis
SOLANIO	John Corvin
BASSANIO	Peter McEnery
LORENZO	Charles Thomas
GRATIANO	Jeffery Dench
PORTIA	Janet Suzman
NERISSA	Patsy Byrne
BALTHAZAR	Tim Wylton
STEPHANO	Ted Valentine
SHYLOCK	Eric Porter
PRINCE OF MOROCCO	Stanley Lebor
LAUNCELOT GOBBO	Charles Kay
OLD GOBBO	Stephen Hancock
LEONARDO	David Quilter
JESSICA	Katharine Barker
PRINCE OF ARRAGON	Donald Burton
SERVANT TO ANTONIO	Robert Walker
TUBAL	Timothy West
MUSICIAN	Martin Best
DUKE OF VENICE	David Waller

SAILORS, MERCHANTS, OFFICERS, LAWYERS, SERVANTS:
Murray Brown, Bruce Condell, William Dysart, Terence Greenidge, Jonathan Hales, David Jaxon, Marshall Jones, Roger Jones, Sylvester Morand, Cliff Norgate, Michael Pennington, David Quilter, Paul Starr, Alan Tucker, John Watts

Number in company	36
Press night	15 April 1965

1971

Director	Terry Hands
Designer	Timothy O'Brien
Costumes	Timothy O'Brien and Tazeena Firth
Lighting	John Bradley
Music	Guy Woolfenden

ANTONIO	Tony Church
SALERIO	Anthony Pedley
SOLANIO	Alton Kumalo
SALARINO	Miles Anderson
BASSANIO	Michael Williams
LORENZO	David Calder
GRATIANO	Geoffrey Hutchings
PORTIA	Judi Dench
NERISSA	Polly James
BALTHAZAR	Michael Shannon
PORTIA'S MAID	Lynn Dearth
SHYLOCK	Emrys James
PRINCE OF MOROCCO	Bernard Lloyd
LAUNCELOT GOBBO	Peter Geddis
OLD GOBBO	Sydney Bromley
LEONARDO	Robert Ashby
JESSICA	Alison Fiske
PRINCE OF ARRAGON	Derek Godfrey
TUBAL	Jeffery Dench
DUKE OF VENICE	Peter Woodthorpe

Number in company	20
Press night	30 March 1971
Transfer	London, Aldwych Theatre, 22 June 1972, with Susan Fleetwood as Portia, Bernard Lloyd as Bassanio, Roger Rees as Gratiano and Lynn Dearth as Nerissa
Audio recording	12 February 1973

1978

Director	John Barton
Designer	Christopher Morley
Lighting	Leo Leibovici
Music	James Walker
ANTONIO	David Bradley
SALERIO	James Griffiths
SOLANIO	Alan Cody
BASSANIO	John Nettles
LORENZO	Paul Whitworth
GRATIANO	John Bowe
PORTIA	Marjorie Bland
NERISSA	Diana Berriman
BALTHAZAR	Dennis Clinton
SHYLOCK	Patrick Stewart
PRINCE OF MOROCCO	Donald Douglas
LAUNCELOT GOBBO	Hilton McRae
OLD GOBBO	Raymond Westwell
JESSICA	Avril Carson
PRINCE OF ARRAGON	Dennis Edwards
TUBAL	Raymond Westwell
DUKE OF VENICE	Dennis Clinton
Number in company	15
Press night	11 May 1978 (The Other Place)
Transfer	London, Warehouse, 2 May 1979

1981

Director	John Barton
Designer	Christopher Morley
Lighting	Brian Harris
Music	James Walker
ANTONIO	Tom Wilkinson
SALERIO	William Armstrong
SOLANIO	John Darrell
BASSANIO	Jonathan Hyde
LORENZO	Michael Siberry
GRATIANO	Arthur Kohn
PORTIA	Sinead Cusack
NERISSA	Corinna Seddon
SERVANT TO PORTIA	Sara Moore
SHYLOCK	David Suchet
PRINCE OF MOROCCO	Terry Wood
LAUNCELOT GOBBO	Rob Edwards
OLD GOBBO	Jimmy Gardner
JESSICA	Judy Buxton
PRINCE OF ARRAGON	Brett Usher
TUBAL	Raymond Westwell
DUKE OF VENICE	Brett Usher
Number in company	16
Press night	21 April 1981
Transfer	London, Aldwych Theatre, 16 July 1981
Audio recording	21 August 1981

1984

Director	John Caird
Designer	Ultz
Lighting	Robert Bryan
Music	Ilona Sekacz

ANTONIO	Christopher Ravenscroft
SALERIO	Jim Hooper
SOLANIO	Ian Mackenzie
BASSANIO	Adam Bareham
LORENZO	Simon Templeman
GRATIANO	James Simmons
PORTIA	Frances Tomelty
NERISSA	Josette Simon
BALTHAZAR	Stephen Simms
STEPHANO	David Phelan
SHYLOCK	Ian McDiarmid
PRINCE OF MOROCCO	Hepburn Graham
GHOST OF PORTIA'S FATHER	Richard Easton
LAUNCELOT GOBBO	Brian Parr
OLD GOBBO	John Rogan
SERVANTS TO BASSANIO	Andy Readman, Jonathan Scott-Taylor
JESSICA	Amanda Root
PRINCE OF ARRAGON	Martin Jacobs
TUBAL	Sebastian Shaw
GAOLER	Andy Readman
DUKE OF VENICE	Richard Easton
CLERK OF THE COURT	Jonathan Scott-Taylor

Number in company	20
Press night	10 April 1984
Video recording	18 January 1985

1986

Director	Roger Michell
Designer	Di Seymour
Lighting	Geraint Pughe
Music	Jeremy Sams

ANTONIO	Paul Webster
SALERIO	David Summer
SOLANIO	William Chubb
BASSANIO	Simon Dutton
LORENZO	Paul Rhys
GRATIANO	Martin Turner
PORTIA	Fiona Shaw
NERISSA	Jacqueline Dankworth
MAID	Susan Harper-Browne
BALTHAZAR	Rupert Holliday Evans
SHYLOCK	Nigel Terry
PRINCE OF MOROCCO	John Bowler
LAUNCELOT GOBBO	Paul McCleary
OLD GOBBO	Dick Brannick
JESSICA	Rachel Joyce
PRINCE OF ARRAGON	Norman Henry
TUBAL	John Bowler
DUKE OF VENICE	Norman Henry
GAOLER	Dick Brannick

Number in company	16
Press night	6 October 1986 (RSC/NatWest tour)

1987

Director	Bill Alexander
Designer	Kit Surrey
Costumes	Andreane Neofitou
Lighting	Robert Bryan
Music	Guy Woolfenden

ANTONIO	John Carlisle
SALERIO	Michael Cadman
SOLANIO	Gregory Doran
BASSANIO	Nicholas Farrell
LORENZO	Paul Spence
GRATIANO	Geoffrey Freshwater
PORTIA	Deborah Findlay
NERISSA	Pippa Guard
BALTHAZAR	Akim Mogaji
STEPHANO	Laban Leake
SHYLOCK	Antony Sher
PRINCE OF MOROCCO	Hakeem Kae-Kazim
LAUNCELOT GOBBO	Phil Daniels
OLD GOBBO	Arnold Yarrow
LEONARDO	David Pullan
JESSICA	Deborah Goodman
PRINCE OF ARRAGON	Richard Conway
TUBAL	Bill McGuirk
GAOLER	David Pullan
DUKE OF VENICE	Richard Conway
OFFICER OF THE COURT	Akim Mogaji
CITIZENS OF VENICE	Henrietta Bess, Susan Harper-Browne, Kate Littlewood

Number in company	21
Press night	29 April 1987
Transfer	London, Barbican, 26 April 1988
Video recording	6 July 1987
Audio recording	29 June 1988

1993

Director	David Thacker
Designer	Shelagh Keegan
Lighting	Clive Morris
Music	Gary Yershon
ANTONIO	Clifford Rose
SALERIO	Richard Clothier
SOLANIO	Tim Hudson
BASSANIO	Owen Teale
LORENZO	Mark Lewis Jones
GRATIANO	Mark Lockyer
PORTIA	Penny Downie
NERISSA	Debra Gillett
BALTHAZAR	David Weston
SHYLOCK	David Calder
PRINCE OF MOROCCO	Ray Fearon
LAUNCELOT GOBBO	Christopher Luscombe
OLD GOBBO	Raymond Bowers
BARMAN	Daniel York
BASSANIO'S ASSISTANT	Johanna Benton
WAITER	Christopher Colquhoun
JESSICA	Kate Duchêne
PRINCE OF ARRAGON	Robert Portal
TUBAL	Nick Simons
SINGER	Tania Levey
DUKE OF VENICE	Christopher Robbie
COURT OFFICER	Stuart Bunce
OFFICERS	Christopher Colquhoun, Daniel York
Number in company	22
Press night	3 June 1993
Transfer	London, Barbican, 8 April 1994
Video recording	13 January 1994
Audio recording	19 April 1994

1997

Director	Gregory Doran
Designer	Robert Jones
Costumes	Sue Wilmington
Lighting	Howard Harrison
Music	Corin Buckeridge

ANTONIO	Julian Curry
SALERIO	Andrew Ufondu
SOLANIO	Andrew Maud
BASSANIO	Scott Handy
LORENZO	Dominic Rowan
GRATIANO	John Dougall
PORTIA	Helen Schlesinger
NERISSA	Siân Reeves
BALTHAZAR	Rowan MacCallum
LADIES	Lisa Reeves, Alexandra Sumner
SHYLOCK	Philip Voss
PRINCE OF MOROCCO	Evroy Deer
LAUNCELOT GOBBO	Jimmy Chisholm
LEONARDO	Alan Stocks
JESSICA	Emma Handy
PRINCE OF ARRAGON	Colin George
TUBAL	Griffith Jones
DUKE OF VENICE	Sandy Macnab
CLERK OF THE COURT	Giles Taylor

Other parts played by members of the company

Number in company	20
Press night	10 December 1997
Transfer	London, Barbican, 8 December 1998
Video recording	11 December 1997
Audio recording	23 February 1999

REVIEWS CITED

1947

Manchester Guardian, 17 July 1947, G.P.
Times, 11 July 1947

1953

Birmingham Mail, 18 March 1953, C.L.W.
Bristol Evening Post, 18 March 1953
Daily Herald, 18 March 1953, Paul Holt
Daily Telegraph, 18 March 1953, W.A. Darlington

1956

Birmingham Gazette, 18 April 1956, Neville Gaffin
Birmingham Post, 19 April 1956, J.G.T.
Bolton Evening News, 21 April 1956, John Wardle
Bristol Evening Post, 18 April 1956, V.M.
Daily Mail, 18 April 1956, Cecil Wilson
Financial Times, 18 April 1956, Derek Granger
Gloucester Echo, 18 April 1956
Leamington Spa Courier, 20 April 1956, F.H.
Oxford Mail, 18 April 1956
South Wales Argus, 18 April 1956, Bill Norris
Stage, 19 April 1956, A.M.
Stratford-upon-Avon Herald, 20 April 1956, Rosemary Anne Sisson
Warwick Advertiser, 20 April 1956, J.A.P.
Yorkshire Post, 18 April 1956, Desmond Pratt

1960

Birmingham Mail, 13 April 1960, W.H.W.
Birmingham Post, 13 April 1960, J.C. Trewin

Daily Mail, 13 April 1960, Robert Muller
Daily Telegraph, 13 April 1960, W.A. Darlington
Evening News, 13 April 1960, David Wainwright
Financial Times, 13 April 1960, Richard Findlater
Guardian, 13 April 1960, Stanley Baker
Liverpool Daily Post, 13 April 1960, N.G.P.
New Statesman and Nation, 23 April 1960
Plays and Players, Peter Roberts
Punch, 27 April 1960
Stage and Television Today, 21 April 1960, Eric Johns
Stratford-upon-Avon Herald, 15 April 1960, Edmund Gardner
Times, 13 April 1960
Yorkshire Post, 13 April 1960, Desmond Pratt

1965

Coventry Evening Telegraph, 17 April 1965, B.J.H.
Financial Times, 17 April 1965, B.A. Young
Observer, 19 April 1965, Penelope Gilliatt
Oxford Mail, 19 April 1965, Don Chapman
South Wales Evening Argus, 19 April 1965, Ken Griffin
Stage and Television Today, 22 April 1965, R.B. Marriott

1971

Birmingham Evening Mail, 31 March 1971
Birmingham Post, 31 March 1971, J.C. Trewin
Coventry Evening Telegraph, 31 March 1971, David Isaacs
Daily Mail, 31 March 1971, Peter Lewis
Financial Times, 23 June 1972, B.A. Young (Aldwych transfer)
Guardian, 31 March 1971, Gareth Lloyd Evans
Shakespeare Survey, 25 (1972), Richard David
Stage, 8 April 1971, R.B. Marriott
Sunday Mercury, 4 April 1971
Sunday Telegraph, 25 June 1972, Frank Marcus (Aldwych transfer)
Sunday Times, 25 June 1972, Harold Hobson (Aldwych transfer)
Times, 1 April 1971, Irving Wardle
Times, 23 June 1972, Irving Wardle (Aldwych transfer)
Yorkshire Post, 31 March 1971, Desmond Pratt

1978

Financial Times, 3 May 1979, B.A. Young (Warehouse transfer)
Shakespeare Quarterly, 30 (1979), Ann Jennalie Cook
Shakespeare Survey, 31 (1978), Roger Warren
Spectator, 12 May 1979, Peter Jenkins (Warehouse transfer)
Times, 15 May 1978, Ned Chaillet
Vogue, July 1979, Marina Warner (Warehouse transfer)

1981

Financial Times, 20 July 1981, Rosalind Carne
Guardian, 23 April 1981, Michael Billington
Jewish Chronicle, 1 May 1981, David Nathan
Jewish Telegraph, 24 December 1980, Marcus Shloimovitz
Sunday Times, 26 April 1981, James Fenton
Times, 18 July 1981, Irving Wardle

1984

Shakespeare Survey, 38 (1985), Nicholas Shrimpton
Times, 11 April 1984, Irving Wardle
Times, 17 April 1984, William Frankel

1987

Country Life, 14 May 1987, Michael Billington
Financial Times, 30 April 1987, Michael Coveney
Times Literary Supplement, 15 May 1987, John Pitcher

1993

Shakespeare Quarterly, 45 (1994), Russell Jackson

ABBREVIATIONS

Birm. E. Mail	*Birmingham Evening Mail*
Birm. E. News	*Birmingham Evening News*
Birm. Gaz.	*Birmingham Gazette*
Birm. Mail	*Birmingham Mail*
Birm. Post	*Birmingham Post*
Bolton E. News	*Bolton Evening News*
Bristol E. Post	*Bristol Evening Post*
Country L.	*Country Life*
Coventry E. Tel.	*Coventry Evening Telegraph*
D. Herald	*Daily Herald*
D. Mail	*Daily Mail*
D. Telegraph	*Daily Telegraph*
E. News	*Evening News*
FT	*Financial Times*
Glos. Echo	*Gloucester Echo*
Jewish Chron.	*Jewish Chronicle*
Jewish Tel.	*Jewish Telegraph*
Leam. Spa Cour.	*Leamington Spa Courier*
Liv. D. Post	*Liverpool Daily Post*
Man. Guardian	*Manchester Guardian*
New States & Nat.	*New Statesman and Nation*
Oxf. Mail	*Oxford Mail*
Plays & P.	*Plays and Players*
SQ	*Shakespeare Quarterly*
SS	*Shakespeare Survey*
S. Wales Arg.	*South Wales Argus*
S. Wales E. Arg.	*South Wales Evening Argus*
Stage & TV	*Stage and Television Today*
SA Herald	*Stratford-upon-Avon Herald*
S. Mercury	*Sunday Mercury*

S. Telegraph	*Sunday Telegraph*
S. Times	*Sunday Times*
TLS	*Times Literary Supplement*
Warwick Adv.	*Warwick Advertiser*
Yorks. Post	*Yorkshire Post*

BIBLIOGRAPHY

Auden, W.H., 'Brothers and others', in *The Dyer's Hand and Other Essays* (London, 1963)

Barber, C.L., *Shakespeare's Festive Comedy* (Princeton, 1959)

Barton, John, *Playing Shakespeare* (London, 1984)

Beauman, Sally, *The Royal Shakespeare Company: A History of Ten Decades* (Oxford, 1982)

Berger, Harry L., 'Marriage and mercifixion in *The Merchant of Venice'*, *Shakespeare Quarterly*, 32 (1981), 155–62

Berry, Ralph, 'Stratford Festival Canada', *Shakespeare Quarterly*, 31 (1980), 167–75

Brown, John Russell (ed.), *The Merchant of Venice*, The Arden Shakespeare (London, 1955)

Bulman, James, *Shakespeare in Performance: 'The Merchant of Venice'* (Manchester and New York, 1991)

Cook, Judith, *Shakespeare's Players* (London, 1983)

Cusack, Sinead, 'Portia in *The Merchant of Venice'*, in Philip Brockbank (ed.), *Players of Shakespeare* (Cambridge, 1985), 29–40

Danson, Lawrence, *The Harmonies of 'The Merchant of Venice'* (New Haven and London, 1978)

Dench, Judi, 'A career in Shakespeare', in Jonathan Bate and Russell Jackson (eds*), Shakespeare: An Illustrated Stage History* (Oxford, 1996), 197–210

Doran, Gregory, 'Solanio in *The Merchant of Venice'*, in Russell Jackson and Robert Smallwood (eds), *Players of Shakespeare 3* (Cambridge, 1993), 68–76

Epstein, Norrie, *The Friendly Shakespeare* (New York, 1993)

Findlay, Deborah, 'Portia in *The Merchant of Venice'*, in Russell Jackson and Robert Smallwood (eds), *Players of Shakespeare 3* (Cambridge, 1993), 52–67

Gaudet, Paul, '"A Little Night Music": intertextuality and status in the nocturnal exchange of Jessica and Lorenzo', *Essays in Theatre/Etudes Théâtrâles*, 13 (1994), 3–14

Granville-Barker, Harley, *Prefaces to Shakespeare*, 2nd series (London, 1948)

Greenwald, Michael L., *Directions by Indirections: John Barton of the Royal Shakespeare Company* (Newark, 1985)

Gross, John, *Shylock: Four Hundred Years in the Life of a Legend* (New York, 1992)

Halio, Jay L. (ed.), *The Merchant of Venice* (Oxford, 1993)

Hapgood, Robert, 'Portia and *The Merchant of Venice*: the gentle bond', *Modern Language Quarterly*, 28 (1967), 19–32

Hyman, Lawrence, 'The rival lovers in *The Merchant of Venice*', *Shakespeare Quarterly*, 21 (1970), 109–16

Leiter, Samuel L., *Shakespeare Around the Globe* (New York, 1986)

Lelyveld, Toby, *Shylock on the Stage* (London, 1981)

Luscombe, Christopher, 'Luscombe on Launcelot', *in RSC Production Pack: The Merchant of Venice* (Stratford-upon-Avon, RSC Education, 1993), 10

Luscombe, Christopher, 'Launcelot Gobbo in *The Merchant of Venice* and Moth in *Love's Labour's Lost*', in Robert Smallwood (ed.), *Players of Shakespeare 4* (Cambridge, 1998), 18–29

McDiarmid, Ian, 'Shylock in *The Merchant of Venice*', in Russell Jackson and Robert Smallwood (eds), *Players of Shakespeare 2* (Cambridge, 1988), 45–54

Mahood, M.M. (ed.), *The Merchant of Venice* (Cambridge, 1987)

Merchant, W. Moelwyn (ed.) *The Merchant of Venice* (London and New York, 1967)

Miller, Jonathan, *Subsequent Performances* (London, 1986)

Shapiro, James, *Shakespeare and the Jews* (New York, 1996)

Smallwood, Robert, 'Directors' Shakespeare', in Jonathan Bate and Russell Jackson (eds), *Shakespeare: An Illustrated Stage History* (Oxford, 1996), 176–96

Stewart, Patrick, 'Shylock in *The Merchant of Venice*', in Philip Brockbank (ed.), *Players of Shakespeare* (Cambridge, 1985), 11–28

INDEX

This index includes actors, directors, critics, and other individuals mentioned in the main text who are connected with a theatre or film production of *The Merchant of Venice*. Individual productions, listed under Shakespeare, are identified by director and year. Page numbers in bold refer to illustrations.

Adams, Polly **89**
Alexander, Bill 22, 55, 56, 57, 58, 132, 148; see also Shakespeare, William, *The Merchant of Venice*
Allen, Patrick **119**, 151
Andrews, Harry **131**
Arnold, Robert **132**
Ashby, Robert 92
Ashcroft, Peggy 19, 20, 95, 122, 125, 127, **128**, **131**, 136
Auden, W.H. 66n.

Bamber, David 47, 49
Barber, C.L. 98
Barton, Anne 19
Barton, John 5, 16, 17, 21, 30, 31, 33, 34, 61, 69, 70, 76, 84, 86, 87, 101, 107, 108, 110, 125, 126, 148, 150, 154; see also Shakespeare, William, *The Merchant of Venice*
Battersby, Julian **97**
Benson, Frank 8
Benthall, Michael 20, 59; see also Shakespeare, William, *The Merchant of Venice*
Berger, Harry L. 98, 99
Berry, Ralph 34
Billington, Michael 128, 129
Bland, Marjorie 21, 35, 84
Booth, Edwin 141, 145
Bowe, John 59, 60, 61
Bradley, David **32**, 47, 131, **133**
Brett, Jeremy 55

Bridges-Adams, William 8, 9
Britton, Tony **131**, 150
Brown, John Russell 12, 13, 24n., 51
Buck, David **119**
Bulman, James C. 9, 57
Buxton, Judy 36, **37**, 39, **155**

Cadman, Michael 50, 56, **65**
Caird, John 22, 154; see also Shakespeare, William, *The Merchant of Venice*
Calder, David 6, **7**, 22, 34, 35, 36, 40, **41**, 42, 109, 110, 114, 115, 116, 135, **136**, 143, 157
Carey, Denis 20, 85; see also Shakespeare, William, *The Merchant of Venice*
Carlisle, John **29**, 55, 58, 85, 138, 152
Carne, Rosalind 61
Carson, Avril 35, 70
Cartwright, Justin 18
Chaillet, Ned 69
Charlesworth, Marigold **128**, **131**
Chisholm, Jimmy 68, 71, 73, 75, 76, 78
Church, Tony 21, 47, **49**, 54, 55, **119**, 133, **134**, 135
Clothier, Richard **136**
Cody, Alan 115, **133**
Conway, Richard 95
Cook, Ann Jennalie 38
Cook, Judith 114, 129

Coryate, Thomas 43n.
Curry, Julian 47, **52**, 58, 130, 134, 152
Cusack, Sinead 19, 21, 81, 82, 84, **88**, 91, 92, 99, 122, 125, 127, 128, **155**

Daniels, Phil 68, 73, **74**
Darlington, W.A. 94, 96
David, Richard 77, 78, 137
Dearth, Lynn 78
Deer, Evroy 94
Dench, Judi 6, 19, 21, **89**, 92, 125, 137, 143, 157
Dignam, Mark 93
Doran, Gregory 23, 42, 50, 56, 63, 64, **65**, 83, 107, 110; see also Shakespeare, William, *The Merchant of Venice*
Dotrice, Roy 21
Downie, Penny 22, 104, 122, 124, 152, 157
Drake, Fabia 99
Duchêne, Kate 36, **41**
Dysart, William **123**

Eagles, Leon **132**
Eason, Myles **60**
Easton, Richard 90
Edwards, Rob **37**, 70, 71, **155**
Elliott, Denholm **119**
Epstein, Norrie 55

Farrell, Nicholas **29**, 50, 55, 57, 101, **102**, 103, 151
Faulds, Andrew **132**, **156**
Fearon, Ray 94
Fenton, James 130
Findlater, Richard 141
Findlay, Deborah 22, 82, 85, 87, 93, 99, **102**, 104, 123, 129, 135, 136, 137, 150, 152, 157
Fiske, Alison 76, **77**
Fleetwood, Susan 92, 125, 150
Frank, Maroussia 96, **97**
Frankel, William 14, 15
Freshwater, Geoffrey 59, **102**

Gaffin, Neville 125
Gardner, Edmund 94
Garley, John 68, 69
Gaudet, Paul 146

Geddis, Peter 69, 76, **77**, 77, 78
George, Colin 95, 98
Gielgud, John 18
Gillliatt, Penelope 54
Godfrey, Derek **89**
Goodman, Deborah 38
Granville-Barker, Harley 8, 80, 81, 98
Greenwald, Michael L. 34
Gross, John 41, 42
Guard, Pippa **102**

Halio, Jay C. 66n., 98, 149
Hands, Terry 12, 21, 116n.; see also Shakespeare, William, *The Merchant of Venice*
Handy, Emma 39, 40
Handy, Scott 47, 50, 51, **52**, 58, 100, 101, 103, 122, 151
Hapgood, Robert 66n.
Hardwick, Paul 93, **94**, 94
Helpmann, Robert 18
Hobson, Harold 76
Holm, Ian 21
Holt, Paul 27
Hoskins, Basil **5**, 46, 47, **132**, **147**, **156**
Howe, George **132**
Hudson, Tim **136**
Hyde, Jonathan 19, 47, 48, **155**
Hyman, Lawrence 66n., 149

Irving, Henry 8, 18, 41, 42, 43, 62, 85, 106, 141, 145; see also Shakespeare, William, *The Merchant of Venice*
Isaacs, David 54

Jackson, Barry 9
Jackson, Russell 100
James, Emrys 19, 21, 28, 37, 107, 112, 115, 116, 133, **134**, 137, 138, 139, 143, 157
Jenkins, Peter 69
Johns, Eric 141
Johnson, Peter **128**, **131**
Johnston, Margaret 20, 122, 125, **132**, **156**
Jones, Mark Lewis **48**
Joyce, Rachel 36, 153

Kae-Kazim, Hakeem 94
Kay, Charles 69, 95, 96

Kean, Edmund 18, 141
Keegan, Shelagh 46
Kingston, Jeremy 7
Kohn, Arthur 155
Koltai, Ralph 54
Komisarjevsky, Theodore 9, 20, 44,
        99; see also Shakespeare,
        William, *The Merchant of
        Venice*
Kumalo, Alton 107

Langham, Michael 20, 45, 141,
        145; see also Shakespeare,
        William, *The Merchant of
        Venice*
Lee, R. Eric 99
Lehmann, Beatrix 20, 157
Leiter, Samuel L. 6
Lelyveld, Toby 42
Lewis, Peter 148
Lloyd, Bernard 47, 55
Lloyd Evans, Gareth 54, 78
Lockyer, Mark 48, 58, 59, 61, 121,
        136
Luscombe, Christopher 67, 68, 72,
        73, 73, 75, 78
Luther, Martin 15

Macklin, Charles 18
Mahood, M.M. 1, 66n., 146
Marcus, Frank 76, 137
Marlowe, Christopher, *The Jew of
        Malta* 16, 21, 68
Marriott, R.B. 54
Maryott, Susan 97, 119
Mason, Brewster 54
Maud, Andrew 109
McCarthy, Mary 15
McDiarmid, Ian 14, 22, 27, 28, 38,
        109, 114, 124, 143, 157
McEnery, Peter 157
McRae, Hilton 69, 70, 71
Merchant, W. Moelwyn 43n.
Michell, Roger 22, 31, 108; see also
        Shakespeare, William, *The
        Merchant of Venice*
Miller, Jonathan 4, 23, 24, 30, 33,
        55, 95, 99, 107, 149, 153;
        see also Shakespeare,
        William, *The Merchant of
        Venice*
Mitchell, Yvonne 147, 147

Mokaji, Akim 102
Moore, Sara 84, 155
Morant, Philip 128, 131
Morley, Christopher 21
Muller, Robert 65

Nettles, John 32, 47
Nicholls, Anthony 5, 46, 47, 55,
        130, 132, 156
Nunn, Trevor 49, 149; see also
        Shakespeare, William, *The
        Merchant of Venice*

O'Brien, David 131
O'Brien, Timothy 148
Olivier, Laurence 4, 23, 24, 30, 33,
        107, 108, 141
Oman, Julia Trevelyan 33
O'Toole, Peter 18, 20, 27, 28, 38,
        65, 96, 109, 111, 112, 113,
        118, 119, 119, 121, 138,
        139, 141

Payne, Ben Iden 8, 9
Payne, Laurence 157
Parker, Joy 60
Parr, Brian 68
Peacock, William 131
Peter, John 6
Pitcher, John 154
Pleasence, Donald 69
Poel, William 9
Porter, Eric 16, 21, 123, 157
Pratt, Desmond 142

Ravenscroft, Christopher 47, 124
Redgrave, Michael 18, 20, 27, 107,
        127, 128, 130, 131
Reeves, Siân 87
Revill, Clive 96
Richardson, Ian 21, 96, 97, 97, 98
Rigg, Diana 21, 84, 97
Roberts, Peter 122
Rose, Clifford 7, 21, 47, 48, 48, 58,
        97, 135, 136
Rowan, Dominic 75
Ruddock, John 20, 37, 157

Scales, Prunella 132, 156
Schlesinger, Helen 87, 87, 95, 99,
        104, 105, 123, 150, 157
Seddon, Corinna 155

Shakespeare, William
As You Like It 125
The Comedy of Errors 68
Hamlet 96, 125
King Lear 78
Love's Labour's Lost 68
The Merchant of Venice directed by
Alexander, Bill, 1987, RSC 11,
12, 17, 19, 22, 27, 28, **29**,
36, 38, 39, 45, 50, 55, 56,
57, 58, 59, 61, 63, 64, **65**,
68, 73, **74**, 74, 82, 85, 87,
88, 89, 92, 93, 94, 95, 99,
101, **102**, 102, 103, 104,
107, 108,110, 114, 115,
116, 119, 120, 121, 122,
123, 129, 130, 131, 132,
135, 136, 137, 138, 139,
140, 142, 148, 150, 151,
152, 153, 154, 157, 169
Barton, John, 1978, RSC 11,
16, 21, 30, 31, **32**, 34, 35,
38, 39, 40, 47, 59, 60, 61,
69, **70**, 70, 71, 76, 84, 86,
87, 101, 107, 108, 110,
111, **112**, 114, 115, 116,
117, 120, 125, 126, 131,
133, 138, 140, 148, 150,
154, 165
Barton, John, 1981, RSC 5, 11,
16, 17, 19, 21, 31, 34, 35,
36, **37**, 37, 39, 40, 47, 48,
61, 69, 70, 71, 76, 81, 82,
84, 86, 87, **88**, 91, 92, 99,
101, 107, 108, 110, 111,
113, 114, 115, 116, 120,
121, 122, 125, 127, 128,
129, 130, 138, 140, 142,
148, 150, 154, **155**, 166
Benthall, Michael, 1947, RSC
11, 20, 37, 42, 59, **60**, 60,
75, 156, 157, 158, 159
Caird, John, 1984, RSC 11, 12,
14, 15, 17, 18, 22, 27, 28,
38, 47, 68, 85, 89, **90**, 90,
104, 105, 109, 114, 124,
142, 143, 154, 157, 167
Carey, Denis, 1953, RSC 11,
20, 27, 69, 75, 83, 85, 95,
107, 122, 125, 127, **128**,
130, **131**, 136, **147**, 147,
150, 160

Doran, Gregory, 1997, RSC
11, 19, 21, 22, 23, 39, 40,
42, 43, 45, 47, 50, 51, **52**,
58, 65, 68, 71, 72, 75, 76,
78, 83, 86, **87**, 87, 88, 92,
93, 94, 95, 98, 99, 100, 101,
103, 104, 105, 107, 108,
109, 110, 112, 113, 114,
115, 118, 120, 122, 123,
130, 134, 137, 138, 140,
141, 143, 148, 149, 150,
151, 152, 155, 157, 171
Hands, Terry, 1971, RSC 6,
11,12, 14, 19, 21, 28, 37,
45, 47, **49**, 54, 55, 63, 69,
75, 76, **77**, 77, 78, 88, **89**,
89, 92, 107, 112, 115, 116,
125, 133, **134**, 134, 135,
137, 138, 139, 143, 147,
148, 149, 150, 153, 156,
157, 164
Irving, Henry, 1879, Lyceum
Theatre, London 8, 41, 42,
43, 62, 85, 106, 141, 145
Komisarjevsky, Theodore,
1932, RSC 9, 20, 44, 99
Langham, Michael, 1960, RSC
11, 13, 20, 27, 28, 38, 45,
65, 75, 84, 88, 93, **94**, 94,
96, **97**, 97, 98, 109, 111,
112, **113**, 118, **119**, 119,
121, 122, 130, 131, 138,
139, 141, 142, 145, 151,
153, 162
Michell, Roger, 1986, RSC 5,
11, 22, 31, 36, 108, 109,
110, 117, 122, **124**, 134,
135, 142, 151, 153, 168
Miller, Jonathan, 1970,
National Theatre, London
4, 23, 24, 30, 33, 47, 55, 95,
96, 99, 107, 108, 141, 149,
153
Nunn, Trevor, 1999, National
Theatre, London 47, 49,
68, 149
Thacker, David, 1993, RSC 5,
6, **7**, 11, 12, 18, 19, 21, 22,
31, 32, 34, 35, 36, 40, 41,
41, 42, 45, **46**, 47, **48**, 48,
49, 58, 59, 61, 62, 65, 67,
68, 72, **73**, 73, 75, 92, 93,

94, 100, 102, 104, 107, 109, 110, 114, 115, 116, 121, 122, 124, 135, **136**, 138, 139, 143, 144, 151, 152, 154, 155, 157, 170

Webster, Margaret, 1956, RSC **5**, 20, 27, 28, 44, **45**, 46, 68, 69, 75, 85, 88, 93, 96, 114, 118, 122, 125, 130, **132**, 142, 155, **156**, 161

Williams, Clifford, 1965, RSC 1, 11, 13, 16, 17, 18, 21, 52, 54, 62, 63, 69, 75, 84, 122, **123**, 131, 152, 153, 157, 163

A Midsummer Night's Dream 68
Much Ado About Nothing 68
Othello 33, 34, 94
Romeo and Juliet 13, 58
The Tempest 94
The Two Gentlemen of Verona 68

Shapiro, James 7, 29
Shaw, Fiona 22, 122, **124**, 151
Shaw, Robert **131**
Sher, Antony 22, 27, 28, **29**, 38, 39, 57, 63, **65**, 107, 108, 110, 114, 115, 116, 119, 121, 135, 138, 139, 157
Shloimovitz, Marcus 16, 17
Siberry, Michael **155**
Simons, Nick **7**, 110
Sinden, Donald **60**
Sisson, Rosemary Anne 68
Smallwood, Robert 10, 153, 154
Squire, William 54, **123**, 157
Sterke, Jeannette **156**
Stewart, Patrick 21, 25, 26, 30, 31, **32**, 34, 35, 37, 38, 39, 41, 108, 110, 111, **112**, 114, 115, 116, 120, 125, 126, 138, 140
Suchet, David 5, 21, 31, 34, 36, **37**, 39, 108, 111, 113, 114, 115, 116, 120, 128, 138, 140, 142
Summer, David **124**
Sumner, David **119**
Surrey, Kit 28
Suzman, Janet 21, 122, **123**, 157
Swift, Clive **113**, 118

Tagg, Alan 20, 44, **45**

Teale, Owen **7**, 47, **48**, 49, 100, **136**, 151
Terry, Ellen 41
Terry, Nigel 5, 22, 109, **124**, 142
Thacker, David 5, 22, 115, 143; see also Shakespeare, William, *The Merchant of Venice*
Tomelty, Frances 22, 104, 105, 124, 157
Tree, Herbert Beerbohm 18, 42
Trewin, J.C. 75, 96
Turner, Michael **131**
Tutin, Dorothy 20, 84, **94**, 96, **97**, **119**, 122, 151

Ufondu, Andrew **109**
Ultz 22, **90**

Valk, Frederick 18
Voss, Philip 21, 22, 39, 43, 107, 108, **109**, 110, 112, 113, 114, 118, **119**, 120, 138, 140, **141**, 143, 157

Wainwright, David 96
Wallace, Ronald **132**
Wardle, Irving 34, 45, 54, 76, 78, 133, 134, 143, 148
Wardle, John 69
Warner, John **60**
Warner, Marina 69, 70
Warren, Roger 38
Webster, Margaret 20, 85; see also Shakespeare, William, *The Merchant of Venice*
Webster, Paul 5, 134
Westwell, Raymond **112**
Wilkinson, Tom 47, 48, 130, **155**
William, David **156**
Williams, Clifford 1, 16, 21; see also Shakespeare, William, *The Merchant of Venice*
Williams, Emlyn **5**, 20, 27, 28, 114, 130, **132**, 142
Williams, Michael 19, 47, **49**, 55, 92, 157
Wilson, Cecil 28
Wilson, Thomas 13, 18
Wood, Terry **88**
Wymark, Patrick **119**

Young, B.A. 54, 61, 69, 125